BEHOLD THE LAMB
...*poetically!*

Behold the Lamb
...*poetically!*
The Birth, Death & Resurrection of Jesus in Poetry

Maude Carolan Pych

ELM HILL
A Division of
HarperCollins Christian Publishing
www.elmhillbooks.com

© 2019 Maude Carolan Pych

Behold the Lamb...*poetically!*
The Birth, Death & Resurrection of Jesus in Poetry

All rights reserved. No portion of this book may be reproduced, stored in a retrieval system, or transmitted in any form or by any means—electronic, mechanical, photocopy, recording, scanning, or other—except for brief quotations in critical reviews or articles, without the prior written permission of the publisher.

Published in Nashville, Tennessee, by Elm Hill, an imprint of Thomas Nelson. Elm Hill and Thomas Nelson are registered trademarks of HarperCollins Christian Publishing, Inc.

Elm Hill titles may be purchased in bulk for educational, business, fund-raising, or sales promotional use. For information, please e-mail SpecialMarkets@ThomasNelson.com.

Scripture quotations marked NASB are from New American Standard Bible®. Copyright © 1960, 1962, 1963, 1968, 1971, 1972, 1973, 1975, 1977, 1995 by The Lockman Foundation. Used by permission. (www.Lockman.org).

Scripture quotations marked NIV are from the Holy Bible, New International Version®, NIV®. Copyright © 1973, 1978, 1984, 2011 by Biblica, Inc.® Used by permission of Zondervan. All rights reserved worldwide. www.Zondervan.com. The "NIV" and "New International Version" are trademarks registered in the United States Patent and Trademark Office by Biblica, Inc.®

Library of Congress Cataloging-in-Publication Data

Library of Congress Control Number: 2019914690

ISBN 978-1-400328031 (Paperback)
ISBN 978-1-400328048 (eBook)

DEDICATION

"Behold the Lamb...*poetically!*" is dedicated with love and a grateful heart to my husband, Bob; to my children, Kristin, Kevin, and Beth Ann; and to the Lamb that was slain, my Risen Savior, Yeshua/Jesus.

> Then I looked and I heard the voice of many angels around the throne and the living creatures and the elders; and the number of them was myriads of myriads, and thousands of thousands, saying with a loud voice, "Worthy is the Lamb that was slain to receive power and riches and wisdom and might and honor and glory and blessing."
>
> And every created thing which is in heaven and on the earth and under the earth and on the sea, and all things in them, I heard saying, "To Him who sits on the throne, and to the Lamb, be blessing and honor and glory and dominion forever and ever." And the four living creatures kept saying, "Amen." And the elders fell down and worshiped.
>
> (Rev 5:11–14 NASB)

TABLE OF CONTENTS

Acknowledgment   xi
Introduction   xiii

The Birth of Messiah   1
The Winged Ones   2
Mary and Elizabeth   5
Greetings, Favored One!   8
Grafted in   11
The Carpenter of Nazareth   13
A Bethlehem Memory   18
What Was God Doing When His Son Was Born?   21
Christmas at the Mall   25
Before the Journey   27
What's This I See?   30
There Was Nothing Cute About It   31
The Christmas Concert   33
My First Christmas Without You   34
Christmases   37
It Was Like Christmas   38
Cookies And Poems   40

Behold the Lamb	42
Wood And Nails	45
The Crèche	47
Setting Up the Manger Scene	50
Littleness	52
The Gift Bearers	54
December Lights	57
The Baby Next Door	59
Revive Us, Dearest Jesus	61
Simeon And Anna	64
Another Silent Night	68
'twas the Night… of All Nights!	70
The Death of Messiah	**73**
Like Mary, at the Feet of Jesus	74
At Chorazin	76
Sometimes I wish	79
Jesus Laughed	81
Mary	84
Imagine	87
Ash Wednesday Reflection	89
Acceptance	91
I'm Not Jewish	93
As the Fall Holidays Approach	96
The Passover Lamb	98
The Name	100
The Lamb	102
About "The Lamb"	105
Love And the Akedah	107
The Binding of Isaac	107

A Poem for Lent	111
The Scrapbook Grandma Made for Me	114
Accustomed to the Cross	117
Paces of a Lamb	119
Between the Palms And the Cross	122
Commemorating the Last Supper	125
Better for Him Had He Not Been Born	127
At the Garden of Gethsemane	131
The Dungeon	134
Pilate's Irony	136
Remembering Good Fridays	138
The Black Bronco	140
Blood Sky Good Friday 2014, Packanack Lake, New Jersey	143
It Pleased the Lord to Crush Him	145
Father, Forgive Them	147
He Refused	149
The Heart-Wrenching Cry	151
The Pieta	153
His Little Lamb	157
At the Via Dolorosa	158
The Circumcised Heart	160
Haiku	163

The Resurrection of Messiah

	165
Beautiful	166
The Place of The Skull	169
What Was God Doing?	171
It's No Wonder	174
Mary of Magdala	178
I've Read the End of the Book	182

A Very Personal Blessing ... 184
Extraordinary Matzoh ... 186
A Better Idea ... 188
He Is Not Here ... 190
Behold the Man ... 192
Holy Face ... 195
Invisible Desecrations Jerusalem Holy Places ... 197
Yeshua ... 200
Risen ... 202
The Emmaus Triptych ... 204
Along Emmaus Road ... 208
Sunflowers Along Emmaus Road ... 211
What Is Truth? ... 213
God's Unfathomable Love ... 216
Acts, Chapter 2 ... 218
Hallelujah Hands ... 221
Mount Scopus ... 223
Marco Sounds the Shofar ... 225
The Little Cupola of the Tablets ... 227
There Are No Words ... 229
I Can't Make You Love Him ... 231
Messianic Believers and Orthodox Jews at the Western Wall ... 233
The Watchman ... 235
Wonderful News ... 236
Biography ... *239*

Acknowledgment

First things first. I will begin by thanking God for enabling me to accomplish my goal of honoring Him with this collection of poetry. I have often felt His hand upon me, providing inspirations and nudging me when decisions needed to be made regarding designing and publishing this book. I humbly thank You, Lord.

Next, I wish to thank the entire staff of Elm Hill Press for bringing the book you hold in your hands to completion, step by step.

Thank you, family, for encouraging me to write and share my poetry openly, with special appreciation to my husband, Robert, for extraordinary patience hour upon hour, day after day, as I sat hunched over the computer.

And to my friend, Rev. E.J. Emerson, the wordsmith, thanks for unfailing help whenever I wrangled with grammar dilemmas.

I am deeply appreciative to Pastors Jonathan Cahn and Stephen Colgate for encouragement over the years. Thank you to the members of the North Jersey Christian Writers Group, my friends in the poetry community, and members of Beth Israel Worship Center, for ongoing support.

Many of the poems in this book have appeared in the present or an earlier version on my website, in chapbooks, and on broadsides. "My First Christmas Without You," "A Very Personal Blessing," and "Wonderful News" appear in my memoir, *Wonderhoods,* published in 2017. "I'm Not Jewish" won third place for poetry in 2010, and "Between the Palms & the Cross" won the Spiritual Award for Poetry in 2019 at St. Catherine of Bologna Festival of the Arts, Ringwood, New Jersey. "My Emmaus," an excerpt from "The Emmaus Triptych," appeared in *The Pillar Monthly.* "Extraordinary Matzoh" was included in William W. Francis' book, *Celebrate the Feasts of the Lord,* Crest Books.

INTRODUCTION

After returning home from my second pilgrimage to the Holy Land in 1987, I wrote my first Christmas poem. It was about standing with our group of pilgrims inside the threshing floor of Boaz near Bethlehem, overlooking the little town. We joyously sang every carol we could think of as one of the music ministers strummed his guitar. "A Bethlehem Memory" was so well received that I continued writing and mailing a new Christmas poem to family and friends every year since. Gradually I began writing poems during Lent, whenever I was inspired by a passage from Scripture and every time I felt prompted by my life journey with Jesus or nudged by the Holy Spirit.

Behold the Lamb...poetically! is a compilation of many of these poems. Some have been published in books and anthologies, some have been presented orally at poetry readings, one is framed and featured with handouts each month at my congregation, and many have been posted on my inspirational poetry blog. I believe creative writing is a gift God has given me to use for His glory, so I do not hide my poems under a bushel, but eagerly share them, always hoping they speak to hearts. I hope they speak to yours.

Please take note of the following: I am an original member (1987) of a then very small but now large Messianic congregation, Beth Israel Worship Center, at the Jerusalem Center in Wayne, New Jersey, where Jew and Gentile worship Jesus, the Messiah, together under the teaching of Pastor/Rabbi Jonathan Cahn.[1] I use the name of Jesus and His Hebrew name, Yeshua, interchangeably in my poetry, and you will find references to Jewish feasts and practices, as well as a sprinkling of Hebrew words throughout. Wherever I think a word requires an explanation, I've inserted parentheses or a footnote.

---

[1] Jonathan Cahn is a Messianic rabbi, biblical scholar, four-time *The New York Times* best-selling author who is best known for his novel, *The Harbinger*.

CHAPTER ONE

THE BIRTH OF MESSIAH

The Winged Ones

Luke 1, NASB

There's a sudden swirl
of fragrance and smoke
as Zacharias tends
the temple altar of incense
Lo! A resplendent angel
appears before his eyes—

It is Gabriel
who stands in the presence of God

The winged one startles the old priest
by proclaiming—

Your wife, Elizabeth, will bear a son…
He will be the forerunner of Messiah

Astonished at the announcement
(for his wife is advanced in years)
Zacharias dares question
God's messenger
and is duly struck dumb—

The Birth of Messiah

and will not utter another word
until the Heavenly proclamation
comes to pass

As gray-haired Elizabeth blossoms
with approaching motherhood
Gabriel alights again
all wings and gleam and glory
in a visit to Mary, a Nazarene maiden
He foretells that she, too, will be with Child—
chosen to be the virgin mother
of the Holy Son of God.

Breathless, Mary runs
to Joseph, her betrothed
eager to tell of the angelic visitation
and Gabriel's marvelous word to her
but it is too much for him to comprehend—
Feeling deceived and disheartened
he considers ending their engagement

until one night, while tossing in sleep
an angel of the Lord appears in a dream
to assure him:
Mary is indeed pure and righteous—
miraculously overshadowed
by the Holy Spirit of God.

so Joseph marries her
and together they await the coming
of the Savior of the World

and when that wondrous event occurs
a multitude of angels fill the Heavenlies
with most glorious splendors
The Bethlehem night becomes brilliant
startling lowly shepherds
reclining in fields with their flocks

and all the beautiful celestial beings
with wings and robes and gladness
proclaim good news of great joy
for *all* people:

Glory to God in the Highest—
Jesus, the Messiah, is born!

Mary and Elizabeth
Ref. Luke 1, NASB

A young virgin
from Nazareth was roused
by the flapping of wings
a man shape in moonbeams
and a perplexing salutation:

Greetings, favored one!
The Lord is with you

It was Gabriel
an angel sent by God
who informed Mary
she would conceive
and bear a boy child, Jesus—
the Son of the Most High

He spoke of the Holy Spirit
and overshadowing
and of her relative, Elizabeth
who though barren
conceived in her old age—

for nothing is impossible with God

Awestruck, trembling
needing to tell someone
who did Mary go to first?
Her mother? Father?
How would they receive such news?
Or did she run to her betrothed, Joseph
expecting him to understand?

Oh, he wanted to understand
wanted to believe, but
it was unbelievable, preposterous
So, stunned, disappointed
feeling utterly deceived, Joseph
contemplated quietly sending her away

Then Mary remembered the angel
had spoken of her dear cousin, Elizabeth—
Is that why Mary hurried off
on a brave trek to the hills of Hebron... alone?
Of course, *it had to be Elizabeth*
aged, wise, expecting
and now acquainted, herself, with miracles

When Mary arrived at the home
of Zacharias and Elizabeth
Elizabeth's unborn baby
leapt for joy in her womb
and in a whirl of wondrous ecstasy
Elizabeth knew of Mary's pregnancy
before being told

The Birth of Messiah

… then a psalm-like lilt of praise
sprang from Mary's lips
extolling the great things
the Mighty One had done for her

Tender were the next three months
as the household awaited Elizabeth's travail
(and the birth of John, the baptizer)

The women prepared their layettes
folded the swaddling clothes
shared their magnanimous miracles
and confided maternal aspirations
as their bellies swelled

… and I like to think
Joseph ran all the way to Hebron
one day expressly to announce
his own angelic vision in a dream—
that he was to take Mary as his wife
and they would await
the miraculous birth of Jesus—*together*

GREETINGS, FAVORED ONE!
Luke 1 and 2; Matthew 2 NASB

I've read the story many times
in the pages of the Gospel of Luke
and many times tried to imagine
exactly how it happened—

tried to picture Mary, as a young virgin
Some sources place her
around the age of my grandchildren
schoolkids about twelve or thirteen

Mary may have been alone in a room
or at the well in Nazareth, drawing water
or with friends in the crowded marketplace
when—

in a moment's whoosh!

a winged man
an angel, Gabriel
from above the highest clouds
the unseen dominions of Heaven
appeared before her
to deliver a vital message
from Almighty God, *Himself!*

THE BIRTH OF MESSIAH

Greetings, favored one! he said

Oh! It's so hard to visualize—

but, I imagine Mary fell prostrate
trembling all over, aware
of each pounding beat of her heart
I imagine she dared not even glance
toward the face of God's holy messenger—

Gabriel likely spoke tenderly
urging her not to be afraid
while explaining
that she would conceive
and bear a Son
He would be called
Jesus, *the Son of God*

Oh! What an astonishing
declaration!

When Mary was finally able to speak
she asked how that could possibly be

and Gabriel told of
the Holy Spirit and overshadowing
by the Lord Most High

BEHOLD THE LAMB...POETICALLY!

Overwhelmed, yet
observant, obedient
and utterly trusting
the Lord, her God

Mary said—
Yes. May it be done unto me
according to God's word.

So, in the fullness of time
miracle of miracles!
the virgin did give birth
in the humblest of places—
a lowly manger
in Bethlehem of Judea

Angels sang *Gloria*
Shepherds left their fields
to worship Him
Magi followed a star
pulsing above them in the sky

Glory to God in the highest—
Jesus, Our Savior, is born!

and the world
has never been the same.

GRAFTED IN

I love to see a Star of David on a Christmas tree,
reminder of my Jewish roots in Christianity.
Happy there is a Hanukiah on a churchyard lawn
adjacent to a manger, dimly flickering at dawn.
I give praise to the Paschal Lamb, crucified at Calvary
Who rose victorious from death to set all sinners free!

I hear a Rosh Hashanah trump forewarning with its cry,
reminding me the Day of God is surely drawing nigh;
then marvel every Yom Kippur at graciousness of God,
lavish with his mercy, He spares the chastening rod.
I read Old Testament prophecy's fulfillment in the New,
with the Messiah's story interwoven through and
    through.

In Shabbat tapers I behold Yeshua, Light of World—
Before my eyes, clearly see, God's glorious plan
    unfurled!
I've been blessed to pray at Israel's Wall and empty
    Tomb
of my Savior, Yeshua, born of Virgin Mary's womb.
At Gethsemane, I've beheld an ancient olive tree
and known within my spirit that one grafted branch
    is me.

Behold the Lamb...Poetically!

I'm born again and spiritually circumcised of heart;
I'm blessed to be a Gentile, who has become a part
of all the covenant promises sealed by the Blood
    of God—
I'll always praise His Holy Name as I walk this
    earthly sod.

THE CARPENTER OF NAZARETH
Matthew 1; Luke 2 NASB

I.

The carpenter laid his hammer down
brushed sawdust from his clothes
slouched onto the crude wooden bench
he'd been working on
and ran calloused hands
through his dark, wavy beard
It seemed he'd misjudged
his beloved, his betrothed
her purity, her fidelity, her forthrightness

Earlier that day
the tender voice he knew well
spoke softly of pregnancy
an angel, overshadowing
of some holy thing
It was too much for him
incomprehensible, even incredible
Joseph leaned back against the rough wood
stretched his sinewy arms
gazed with resignation toward the heavens
He'd hand her a bill of divorcement—
wash his hands. It was over. Finished
He rose, shook his head
and returned to work

In the night
tension dissolved
into welcome sleep
Deep in its midst
a flurry of wings and light
wrapped him in wonder
A stirring voice resonated:

Fear not…
Take Mary as your wife

Words whirled as he tossed:

for the Son conceived in her
is of the Holy Spirit.

Then distinctly, Joseph heard:

Name Him Jesus…
He will save your people from their sins.

II.

Mary placed a few belongings into a sack—
She and Joseph were about to leave
for Bethlehem, for the census
She felt a hardy kick
from inside her swollen belly
and reflexively caressed the spot

The Birth of Messiah

A knee, she smiled

God had chosen her for a purpose
she could barely comprehend
and the birth would be soon
She neatly folded soft, clean cloths
and packed them
just in case her time would come
during the journey

Traveling was arduous
by foot and donkeyback
over hills and rocky terrain
Joseph was attentive
stopping periodically for rests
but evening was fast approaching
Finally, they could see the town ahead
Suddenly, Mary felt her stomach stiffen
Was this the sign
Elizabeth had told her about?
Her back ached. She was weary
Soon, her stomach tightened again
then again, but stronger
She alerted Joseph
who touched her, tenderly
and bid her not to fret
Lodging was close by
but when they arrived
the innkeeper told them

the place was packed with travelers
Seeing their dilemma
he offered shelter and privacy
in the livestock cave out back
Joseph helped her off the donkey
and into the dark rock-hewn cave
Hurriedly, he gathered fresh hay
and prepared a makeshift nook
apart from the animals
then sat at Mary's side, cooling her brow
as contractions intensified

III.

In the evening chill
amid moon and star and lantern light
the musky odor of straw and dung
rhythmic sounds of
braying, bleating
and occasional shouts and laughter
emanating from the inn,
the carpenter rolled his sleeves
and delivered the Promised One
The healthy wail of a baby boy
filled them with joy
Joseph presented the Child
to his virginal wife to nurse
then emptied a rugged old trough
and filled it with sweet-smelling hay
all the time thinking

of the fine, smoothly sanded cradle
back home in Nazareth

Jesus, someday I'll teach you
how to select the finest woods
how to build and saw and sand
You'll be a fine carpenter, Jesus
a very fine carpenter....

Joseph carefully placed Jesus
in the makeshift cradle
then fashioned a spot for himself
on the floor of the cave
and soon fell fast asleep

A Bethlehem Memory
Israel Pilgrimage II, May 1987

O little town of Bethlehem
how still we see thee lie
from the wheat field of Boaz
one pleasant mid-spring night

A zealous band of pilgrims
tracing footsteps of the Lord—
with hearts ablaze to praise
One so worthy to be adored

We huddle at a circular
stone threshing floor for wheat
with eyes fixed on the little town
so Christmas tableau sweet

We look around for shepherds
as the sun is going down
while to the strumming of guitar
we lift the joyful sound

of our voices unto Heaven
to give our gift of song...
Every carol that we know
is offered by the throng

The Birth of Messiah

The evening is so glorious
we do not want to leave—
Our dinners may be getting cold
but here our spirits cleave

The darkness slowly deepens
as dim starlight appears...
twilight glows with hymn song
while in reverie we veer

back to the old, old stories
of the night of Holy Birth
while being so enthralled by
this blessed bit of earth

In the distance, the townsfolk
begin to light their lights
for the routine of living
in this simply awesome site

We wonder, do they ever kneel
to kiss the hallowed ground
where they spend their every days?
Do the amber fields resound

with ecstatic jubilation?
Do stars shoot sparks of praise
for the glorious Gift given
that precious day of days?

Behold the Lamb...Poetically!

O little town of Bethlehem...
this night we'll always treasure
Echoes of carols, memories
will remain forever

Pure joy overflows our hearts
for Bethlehem's Babe, Our Lord,
was born *here* to save sinners...
Jesus, Savior of the World!

WHAT WAS GOD DOING WHEN HIS SON WAS BORN?

What was God doing?
What was He thinking
high up in His Heaven
when He sent the angel
to the virgin to tell her
about overshadowing
and childbirth
and salvation for the world?

What was God doing?
What was He thinking
high up in His Heaven
when in great anguish
Joseph didn't believe his betrothed
and was about to call off their union
until in a dream he realized
they were a part
of an awesome and holy plan?

What was God doing?
What was He thinking
high up in His Heaven
when heavy with child

Behold the Lamb...Poetically!

Mary traveled with Joseph
by donkey in the dust and hills
clip-clopping to Bethlehem
for the census
and once there,
couldn't find a proper place
for them to stay
and time for the travail
had come?

What was God doing?
What was He thinking
high up in His Heaven
when in a cool cave
with livestock and hay
and dung and dampness
Joseph helped his wife
bring forth the Child
with rugged, splintered hands?

What was God doing?
What was He thinking
high up in His Heaven
when Joseph held the Babe
Heavenward, in thanksgiving
and blessing, then presented
Him to Mary,
who called Him Jesus
and nursed Him at her breast?

THE BIRTH OF MESSIAH

What was God doing?
What was He thinking
high up in His Heaven
when Mary wrapped Jesus
in swaddling cloths
and placed Him in fresh hay
her husband prepared
in a crude wooden trough?
What, oh what
was God thinking
looking down from His Heaven
upon His only begotten
born into the world
as the Least
and the Most?

What was God doing?
What was He thinking
high up in His Heaven?
Did He celebrate with the angels
before sending them Earthward
with their jubilant Glorias
and triumphant trumpets?
Did His joy set ablaze
the beckoning star above Bethlehem?
Did He preen with pure pride
as shepherds and kings
came bearing their gifts?

Did He shudder an Almighty shudder
high up in His Heaven
at the movement toward fruition
of His cosmic plan?
Did He see flashes of thorns
and spikes and tree,
flashes of Blood
washing sin? In the dark stillness,
as Joseph and Mary
fell into exhausted sleep,
did God reach quietly down,
chuck Jesus' chin,
and whisper in His tiny ear,

You have Your Father's eyes,
My Son.

CHRISTMAS AT THE MALL

Day after Thanksgiving, at the mall, what is this
    I see...
Santas sledding in the air and a tinseled
    Christmas tree,
a roly-poly Frosty, red-nosed Rudolph with some
    elves,
glittery garlands, balls, and bows, bedazzling on the
    shelves?
The shops are alive with music, "White Christmas,"
    "Jingle Bells";
there are *Ho, ho, hos*, *Let It Snows* and cinnamony
    smells.

It certainly all seems festive, so cheery and so bright,
but what oh what does it have to do with that holy
    night?
I cannot find a manger scene, an angel, or a star,
I do not see the wise men... wonder where the
    shepherds are.
I do not hear a carol or the story of the birth
of our dear Lord Jesus, Who saved sinners here on
    Earth.

Some, it seems, have cast aside the things that
    matter most—

Behold the Lamb...Poetically!

By replacing Truth with fairytales, Treasure has
    been lost.
My heart fills up with sorrow and causes me to prod
the fading faith of loved ones who used to walk
    with God.
Lord, help us to remember the virgin and the Child...
Revive in us once strong faith that's been waning a
    while.

BEFORE THE JOURNEY
Luke 2 NASB

Sitting quietly in the dim glow of an oil lamp
trying to get comfortable
in the sturdy wooden armchair
made by her carpenter husband,
Mary rests both hands
upon her taut, round stomach
and smiles at the gentle rumbling within—
the Son of God in utero

Although this is centuries before sonograms,
Mary knows her babe is a boy child
and that they are to name Him Jesus—
for an angel told her so

Young and bewildered, she wonders
what her holy Son will look like and be like
if he'll want to work with wood
She wonders about the cosmic plan
set in motion by her "yes"
and how a Savior saves

She dares not dwell too deeply
upon what lies ahead

and why so lowly a maiden as she
would be highly favored
by the Lord her God

but she trusts Him
... and she's obedient

Joseph is a righteous man—
She watches as he sands smoothly
the fine cradle he is building
and appreciates that he stands by her
shielding her from questions, innuendos
finger-pointers and gossipmongers

Their donkey is tied outside
the humble dwelling in Nazareth
She hears it braying and nuzzling at the door

It'll go with them tomorrow
on their journey to Bethlehem
where they must register
for the census

She sighs, thinking of the long
arduous journey
especially in her condition

Well, I'd better get some rest

The Birth of Messiah

she tells Joseph
as she rises awkwardly from the chair
and carries the lamp closer
to where her husband is working

I've packed a bundle of swaddling clothes
… just in case

What's This I See?

Exodus 12:21–23 NASB
1 Corinthians 5:7 NIV

What's this I see in a feeding trough?
A Lamb asleep in a bed of straw
without any blemish to behold...
the Lamb deserves a crown of gold

What's this upon crossbeams, I see?
A Lamb impaled... sacrificially!
I fall to my knees before His Grace—
the Lamb looks down. *I see God's face*

From lintels stained with blood of lambs
to the Cross that saves from being damned—
the whole Word holds a mystery... *deep!*
the Blood of the Lamb saves His sheep

All glory to our Paschal Lamb
Messiah, Son of the great I AM
Who from that humble bed of straw
became our Savior... *We bow in awe!*

THERE WAS NOTHING CUTE ABOUT IT
Luke 2 and Matthew 2 NASB

When Mary traveled with Joseph
from Nazareth to Bethlehem
over ruts and rocks and hills
jostled on the back of a donkey
during her final day of pregnancy,
it was an arduous journey—
There was *nothing cute about it*!

And when her labor pains began
and she was far from home,
far from the midwife she trusted
and the birthing room turned out to be
the hay-strewn floor of a dirty stable,
there was *nothing cute about it*!

And when following the birth of Jesus
Joseph had a dream
and determined they had to flee to Egypt
to escape Herod's twisted plan
so they quickly tossed a few necessities
in a saddle-bag and the three of them set off
for a place of safety—
there was *nothing cute about it, at all*!

But, when I open my pretty Christmas cards
and see the holy family journeying
with Mary, draped in a lovely blue gown,
and Joseph strolling alongside her
staff in hand, as their donkey
plods along agreeably,
it all looks pleasant and serene

and when I gaze at manger scenes
(including my own)
arranged tidily on polished tabletops,
the scene is as perfectly charming
as the annual Christmas tableau
at Radio City Music Hall

still, the reality is—
There was nothing cute about it!

Oh, but wasn't the fact
that the miracle happened
absolutely astonishing
just the same?

THE CHRISTMAS CONCERT

As a mother and a father sit with other moms and dads
in a crowded auditorium waiting for their gals and lads

to perform at the Christmas concert playing flute or sax or drum
or caroling their hearts out, parents sit smiling, rapt and mum.

It doesn't matter if their offspring forget some words or squeaks;
parents just keep snapping photos. This is one of life's sweet peaks!

Observing, it occurred to me, when I give God stammered praise
or fumble with lyrics of a hymn, His eyes do not get glazed.

My prayer need not be eloquent; my song need not be smooth.
God's tender eyes are watching me; there is nothing I must prove.

As each loving mom and dad adore their child's song, off-key
my Heavenly Father knows my heart. He's pleased to hear from me!

My First Christmas Without You

This poem was written following the death of my husband, Leo F. Carolan, in 2004.

Wrote my annual Christmas poem
and sent it out as usual
well aware that anyone who didn't already know
would know even before they opened it
as soon as they saw the return address label
with just my name on it—
Included your photograph
and a few words about your passing
baby photos of Logan and Aiden
and a few words about God taketh and giveth

Shopped, pretty much as usual
except, of course, that a significant gift
was missing from my list
I gift wrapped, set up the crèche
and hung a few decorations
Baked cookies—
shortbread, chippers,
anise biscotti, sugar cookie stars

Packed tins to mail
and give and have on hand.

The Birth of Messiah

I'd glance at the empty chair
and miss you sitting there, smiling
as I rolled out dough
and sang "O Holy Night" way off-key

Received lots of cards
and lots of notes and phone calls
from people stunned
by the news in my letter

Beth and Evert invited me to spend
the day before Christmas Eve with them
before they flew to Miami
with Logan to visit Evert's mom

On Christmas Eve I went to Beth Israel
to celebrate the birth of Messiah
Gave Pastor Jonathan his tin of cookies
then headed south on the Parkway
after midnight so I could be
at Kristin and Randy's in time
to see Aiden's eyes light up his first
Christmas morning

Over the next few days
I visited my sister and brother,
Aunt Carol, and friends

Behold the Lamb...Poetically!

Kevin and Omayra invited me
to spend a quiet New Year's Eve
with Omy's family in South River
Tearless, pensive, I lifted a glass
to ring out the old, ring in new
I slept in the guest room
at my son and daughter-in-law's home
We sat around the table in our bathrobes
New Year's Day morning, eating
buttered panettone with glazed chestnuts
then drove to The City
to see the play, *Golda*
We ate in a deli that charged holiday prices
and toured Ground Zero on foot

then
it was over
I got through it

without going to pieces

CHRISTMASES

There have been Christmases
when we hung the garland
and shopped and partied
and tried to force festive smiles
while our broken hearts
wanted to hide in solitude
because a parent died
or there was illness
or the marriage
was falling apart

There have been Christmases
we wanted to cut
out of the calendar
even though
Jesus was worthy
of our fullness

He understood
even if we didn't, then

Ah, but this
is a Christmas of joy…
We shop with enthusiasm
We sing carols as we trim
and our hearts dance
as we praise Him mirthfully

We're healed
and Christmas is a wonder

IT WAS LIKE CHRISTMAS

*Every good and perfect gift is from above,
coming down from the Father of the heavenly
lights, who does not change like shifting
shadows.*

(JAMES 1:17 NIV)

Perhaps it was a vision
or at least a vivid imagining...
It was like Christmas!
There was a great heap of presents
of various sizes,
gaily wrapped,
tied with streaming ribbons
and lustrous bows,
each with a gift tag
that bore my name.
Some presents
had already been opened,
wrappings strewn, white tissue awry,
others, wonderfully enticing,
were yet to be unwrapped.

In my spirit I knew
they were gifts of God,
the spiritual blessings

The Birth of Messiah

of my life.
The open ones
represented gifts already acquired.
Some bedazzled,
those, the granted yearnings
of the prayers of my heart,
others were blessings also
though never sought in prayer,
still others were gifts
I *never* wanted,
gifts I'd have preferred
to return or exchange.
In time I understood
each was perfect,
selected by the Source
of all wisdom
with me alone in mind,
loving graces
spiritually working in me
creating the me
I am becoming in Him.
I look to the future
anticipating
wondrous gifts
still unopened.

COOKIES AND POEMS

*In 2006, Robert F. Pych and I were married.
Bob is the one mentioned in this poem who gladly
assists with the mailing of Christmas poems and
the baking of Christmas cookies.*

So many Christmas traditions abound—
Old ones get lost and then new ones are found.
Some get omitted, but there are a few
things we love doing and simply must do.

For instance, I write a poem every year—
a real Christmas poem that draws Jesus near;
a poem that lauds Him, Star of the Season,
for He's this holiday's only true reason.

The poem's perfect paper, I search far to find,
arrange words artistically as I've in mind,
select address labels with the same theme,
choose envelopes, stamps that go with the scheme.

The pen and the ink are chosen with care.
To use best penmanship, I have a flair!
I write out hundreds with joy and much zest
and sometimes include a few words to bless.

The Birth of Messiah

Bob applies the stamps and labels and seals;
a trip to the post office completes the deal.
When they're mailed, I start thinking cookies—
Trust me, with baking, I am no rookie!

We select recipes, gather the tins,
make sure there's flour and sugar in bins,
stock up on butter and chocolate and nuts,
molasses and spices and trims lots and lots!

I block off a few days in my datebook,
roll up my sleeves, open up the cookbook.
Chocolate chippers, and shortbread sooooo buttery,
sweet sugar cookies, anise biscotti,

spicy pfeffernuesse and wee pecan jewels,
drop cookies, rolled cookies, some cut with tools.
Bob stirs the batters; they're thick as can be
and he's the chief taster, take it from me!

Each cookie and poem is fashioned with love—
LOVE is what Christmastime is made up of.
God's gift of LOVE came with the Savior's birth
and there's no other gift of greater worth!

These simple gifts... some cookies, a poem,
for Christmas, to you, from our humble home.

BEHOLD THE LAMB

Leviticus 22:17–20 NASB
John 1:29 NASB

I.

In a grassy field in Bethlehem
a rugged old shepherd
tenderly smooths the wooly coat
of a pregnant ewe, as she bleats in labor
almost ready to deliver her offspring

He's been through this many times—
Patiently, the shepherd remains with her
prepared to assist as she gives birth

Immediately following the delivery, he wisely wipes
the membrane away from the lamb's face
so it can breathe, while the mother
instinctively licks it all over with her tongue
In a few minutes, it rises on wobbly legs
and manages a few shaky steps

Then the shepherd picks it up
and carefully examines
every limb and joint and crevice
Finding no blemish

THE BIRTH OF MESSIAH

he wraps strips of swaddling cloth
around its delicate little hooves
to protect them from splintering or cracking

He'll raise this spotless little lamb
with utmost care—

and present it to the Levitical priests
designated for sacrifice
upon the altar at the Temple in Jerusalem

as an atonement for sin

II.

The old shepherd
warms himself by the fire
with the younger men
when suddenly the sky is alight
with angels singing praises to God
and announcing with joy
the birth of Yeshua (Jesus), Savior of the World

Filled with great jubilation,
the shepherds set off
with their flock, to honor Him
They don't have far to travel

In a lowly stable outside an inn
they find the Babe

with His mother, Miriam (Mary)
and her husband, Yosef (Joseph)

Baby Yeshua is without blemish
swaddled and sleeping, in a makeshift cradle
that is actually a feeding trough for animals

Years go by
and in the fullness of time
the Man, Yeshua, presents Himself
to Yochanan (John), the Baptizer,
on the shore of the Jordan River

As He approaches
Yochanan proclaims to all who will listen—

*Behold the Lamb of God
who takes away the sin of the world!*

A few years later
Yeshua, Son of God, the spotless Lamb,
does exactly that, once and for all—

at the Cross

WOOD AND NAILS
Matthew 27:51 NASB

I.

His splintered hands sand silky smooth
every ding and bump and groove;

then Joseph measures every piece—
hammers nailheads with expertise.

He's built fine cradles, but this one
is extra special. *It's for God's Son.*

He moves Babe Jesus from the trough
to the cradle, cushioned and soft.

The manger scene, quaint and lowly,
now more befits One Who's holy.

Joseph, years hence will reap a thrill—
He'll teach the boy carpentry skills.

II.

Shoved on crossbeams, Jesus' body.
Crude wood. Workmanship is shoddy.

Behold the Lamb...Poetically!

Men grab His wrists. They pound the nails.
They watch Him wince; His color pales.

They lift the Cross, taunt till He dies.
The air is pierced by women's cries.

The sky grows dark. The dry earth quakes.
O hear the hissing of the Snake...

Then...

Holy of Holies veil is torn—
Sin is atoned! Salvation born!

God's Master Plan, now understood—
began and ends with nails and wood.

THE CRÈCHE

I was a bride of twenty in the mid-sixties
decorating my home creatively and economically
by attending ceramic classes Tuesday evenings
in Bette Carozza's basement
We sat around the table with coffee cups
cleaning greenware, applying
underglazes and overglazes
speaking girl talk all the while
We made cookie dishes and ashtrays
glossy green Christmas trees with snowy branches
fitted with tiny colored lights
We made rooster lamps, pitchers and bowls,
piggy banks, and tall German beer steins
The most ambitious of us
made chess pieces and Nativity figures

I began working on my Nativity set in 1965
took a few months off after Mom died
and picked up the last pieces
hot from Bette's old electric kiln
on Christmas Eve Day, 1966
How well I recall carefully cleaning
the fragile greenware with a sharp tool
till the seams were perfectly smooth
sanding and sponging tiny bumps
and filling pit holes

Behold the Lamb...poetically!

Wanting to be as authentic as possible
I applied three coats of sky blue to Mary's robe
(Did Mary actually own a blue robe?)
and ruddy brown to Joseph's tunic
Jesus' features were less sharp
than the other figures
having been cast from a mold
that had been poured too many times
I made the flesh tones too pale
for Middle Easterners
The magi and their regal camels
were embellished with accents of pure gold
and I even glued tiny rhinestones
onto their gift offerings
even though it's likely
the wise men didn't visit the Christ Child
until months after He was born
The shepherds' garb were given earth tones
and a staff was provided for one of them
fashioned from a birch twig
I dabbed white froth onto the lambs' coats
and gave the cow big brown patches
making it a Guernsey,
a breed not likely to have grazed
the fields of Bethlehem.
The long-eared donkey was painted gray
Bette's husband, ChiChi,
built a fine wooden crèche
with a hook on top
to hang the golden-haired angel
who flourished a banner proclaiming

The Birth of Messiah

"Gloria in Excelsis Deo"
I installed a music box
which played "Adeste Fideles"
and a little light bulb
and bought a bag of sweet straw
from Woolworth's

For more than five decades now
a few weeks before Christmas
I've been unpacking the big cardboard box
unwrapping the fragile figures from newspaper
and displaying them throughout the season.
When the children were young
Jesus wasn't placed in the manger
until Christmas Eve
when we all gathered round
and sang, "Happy Birthday"

The angel now has a chipped wing
and the Guernsey's missing a horn
but Jesus still lies sweetly in His crib
apparently not minding whether or not
I managed to get every jot and tittle
of His manger scene historically correct
He just lies sweetly there
year after year
reminding us
that significant night
long, long ago
is a forever celebration

Setting Up the Manger Scene

A few snowflakes drift in wintry air
as I carry the carton down the stairs
and unwrap the antique fragile things—
a manger, some camels, and three kings.

I set them on the polished tabletop,
being careful not to chip or drop
them as I do. Sheep and shepherd men
are arranged as entering Bethlehem.

An angel, gilded, with one chipped wing,
is affixed above, her place to sing.
There's a cow and donkey, nibbling straw,
Joseph, kneeling, with a look of awe

and Mary, new at being mother,
gazing adoringly at none other
than her swaddled, holy, infant Son…
Jesus, Our Savior, on day one.

As I move each figure to its place,
I call upon God's loving grace…
pray each who stand before my manger,
to Jesus, will *never* be a stranger.

The Birth of Messiah

May this heirloom crèche, made long ago,
recall the event that sets hearts aglow.
May He be for them, as He's been for me—

Sweet Love...
for now
and through eternity.

LITTLENESS

In a little manger, in a little town,
was born a little Boy,
to a little family of little means.
He brought the world great joy!

If the Lord of All could come so small,
with the biggest, highest aim,
then why oh why must we buy and buy
for the day that bears His Name?

We shop, we trim, we bake, we cook,
we visit, we send, we party,
we run up the tally on credit cards,
the bills we pay are tardy.

While the hustle and bustle can be great fun,
sometimes it steals our peace,
sometimes the true Christmas spirit gets lost
when our busyness won't cease.

From the little manger, the little town,
the crib of the little Boy,
comes a little Christmas thought to muse,
which may heighten Christmas joy....

The Birth of Messiah

Let us celebrate with *littleness*,
become as the little Child,
with simplicity, wonder, innocence,
pure Love that's undefiled...

and the Savior, Our Lord, who was that Child,
shall smile at us, well pleased,
For the kingdom, He said, *of Heaven belongs
to people such as these!*

The above poem was inspired by a message delivered by Pastor/Rabbi Jonathan Cahn, at Beth Israel Worship Center.

THE GIFT BEARERS
Matthew 2

Cosmic wonders, whats and whys
whirl in the East
as a singular mysterious luminary
beckons in the heavens.
Is it brighter than the other stars?
Does it pulsate? Does it bounce?
Does it shoot across the sky
like a flame-tailed comet?
Does its lustrous splendor
rival the glow of the moon?

Gentile magi who study stars and Scripture
see it and curiously mount their camels
to follow it across the desert. But, why?
They say they are seeking
the King of the Jews. Why would they?
They say they want to worship Him
Why Him?
What do they know that the High Priest
the Pharisees, Sadducees,
and all the Jews of Jerusalem
who are awaiting the coming of Messiah
do not comprehend?

The Birth of Messiah

King Herod summons them, diabolically
Feigns sincere interest in their mission
urges them to return with details
so he, too, may worship the King
A sinister plot forms in his evil mind
for even he knows...
there is *something* about that star...

Continuing on,
the irresistible starlight shines ahead
until it shimmers above a humble house
in the village of Bethlehem
It stops, still... absolutely still
The magi realize they are at
Destiny's door
They knock
and are welcomed, when

Suddenly
their eyes behold
a Boy Child
and their hearts leap!!!

And whether it makes sense or not
(whether any of this makes sense or not)
the magi, in rich array,
fall prostrate
on the earthen floor
and fill the little house
with Hallelujahs!!!

Behold the Lamb...poetically!

They draw from their saddlebags, treasures...
Gold... for surely this little family can use it
Myrrh... fragrant foreshadow of suffering
Frankincense... for a sensing in the depths
of their God-given wisdom
of a significant anointing
somewhere in time

Mission complete,
the gift bearers mount their camels
and still attentive to God's spirit
(this time in a dream)
do not return to Herod

The magi...
diligent seekers who found
Treasure
infinitely more valuable
than the precious gifts they bore

DECEMBER LIGHTS
Romans 11 17–27

It's the Season of Lights....We delight in the glow
of Christmas and Hanukkah, the stories we know
of God's awesome miracles, deliverance and Birth
to show His great Love for all people on Earth.

Alongside our manger there stands a menorah;
we sing "Joy to the World" and then dance the hora,
ignite the nine lamps and hang a wreath on the door,
tell of brave Maccabees, Messiah's birth, and more.

We worship with believers, Gentiles and Jews,
we recite the Shema and share the Good News,
read Old Covenant prophesies from A to Z
like the Gospel revealed in Isaiah Fifty-Three!

Our Messiah is Jesus; Yeshua, some say—
He's the Light of the World, our great hope for today!
We praise Him, adore Him, we're blessed to impart:
His fire burns brightly in our circumcised hearts!

We believe He was born to save us from sin,
that He died and was buried then rose up again.

Behold the Lamb...Poetically!

**By Blood He has saved us, our Atonement, He Is!
By His Resurrection, we'll live for He Lives!**

**We are Olive Tree branches, Gentile and Jew—
natural and grafted in... we are all Born Anew!**

THE BABY NEXT DOOR

I saw him the other day
the baby boy who lives next door
His parents are poor Hebrews, like we are
He's swaddled the same way we swaddle our babies
and he cries and coos just like our babies do, yet—

the brightest star I've ever seen
shines down upon *him* every night
and shepherds have left their fields
just to take a look at *him*
exclaiming all the while
about angels singing in the sky

Really? Angels in the sky—

One day I saw wise men from afar
dressed in finery, ride in on camels
They were bearing costly gifts to honor him
and actually bowed prostrate
before his little cradle

BEHOLD THE LAMB...POETICALLY!

I met his mother at the well, yesterday
Her name is Miriam (Mary)
She told me they've named him, Yeshua (Jesus)

Yeshua is a fine name. It means savior
Savior. We've been waiting for a savior—

Hmmmmm...

REVIVE US, DEAREST JESUS

My Christmas Prayer for Revival in America
2 Chronicles 7:14

The morning sun is streaming in as I prepare to pray
recalling what my pastor said in his word to us
    one day.
He spoke of the time we live in and of people losing
    faith,
of disregard for God's Holy Word, and an increase
    in hate.

Many churches are closing or the Gospel gets
    watered down,
there's disrespect for spiritual things, and God is
    made a clown.
My pastor said he's burdened; therefore he's asking
    us to pray
for a nationwide revival, hope for all who've gone
    astray.

Oh, my dear Lord Jesus, You were born to save us,
    this I know,
and by Your death upon the Cross, You conquered
    the evil foe.

I know Your desire is that none be lost, that's my
     desire, too;
therefore, I am humbly on my knees and crying out
     to You,

to reveal to all who know You, Lord, the need to
     repent.
Point us back to Your Holy Cross and why Your
     Blood was spent.
America must turn back to You and live our lives
     Your way.
Oh! Let there be revival here. Let us see it in
     our day!

We must have sorrow for our sins and confess those
     sins to You.
We need to call upon Your Name and then be
     Born Anew.
Through Your amazing grace and love, there'll be
     splendors in store
and by Your Resurrection, we will have life
     forevermore!

May multitudes flock unto You, countless as grains
     of sand.
May churches fill up with faithful folks all across
     our land.
May dusty Bibles be opened and hearts abound
     with love.

The Birth of Messiah

Lord, I'm sending this Christmas prayer, straight to
>   Your throne above.

O Savior, You are worthy to receive our honor and
>   praise.
Draw the backsliders, draw the lost, to walk in all
>   Your ways—
Revive! Revive us, Jesus! I long to see what You will do
in answer to this earnest prayer… all glory belongs
>   to You!

Simeon And Anna
Luke 2: 22–40 NASB

Simeon wondered
if he were seeing things
He rubbed his tired old eyes
squinted and peered again
at the little family
that came through the Temple doors

The Sanctuary
was shadowy and dim
Flames from the oil lamps flickered—
Were his eyes playing tricks?

Wasn't this an ordinary family?
... a couple like any
ordinary Jewish couple
here to present their firstborn son
holy to the Lord?

Nothing special about them
Just poor folk
with two lowly turtledoves
for the sacrifice... yet?

The Birth of Messiah

Perhaps this was wishful thinking
Perhaps, his imagination
He needed to be sure
Simeon moved a bit closer

Oh, he'd been waiting so patiently
for the fulfillment of the promise
of the Lord to comfort Israel

He knew He would—
for the Holy Spirit
assured him
he absolutely would not die
until he beheld the Messiah
… but that was long ago

Suddenly an unmistakable quickening
began rising up in his spirit… *Yes!*
… *O Glory! Glory!*

He bounded
toward Mary and Joseph
with arms outstretched
and swooped up
their swaddled infant Son
uttering prophetic proclamations
jubilant and terrifying:

I behold God's salvation!

Behold the Lamb...Poetically!

A light to the Gentiles

The glory of God's people Israel

and directly to Mary, he prophesied:

... a sword will pierce your soul

She shuddered...
for she knew God had a plan, but...
What could this mean?

Then the widow Anna approached
Bent and gray and pious
she was a prophetess
who dwelled in the Temple
most of her life, praying
fasting and serving the Lord
with a joyful heart

Spontaneous praise
sprang from her lips
as she beheld the Babe
Then Anna proclaimed
to all who would listen:

Come and see...
This is our Newborn Redeemer!

The Birth of Messiah

... from that day forward
Jesus grew
in wisdom and grace

the Cross before Him...

... and a sword did pierce
Mary's soul

ANOTHER SILENT NIGHT

Luke 2: 22–33 NASB

My friend Holly (who has a special
affinity with all things Christmas)
once gave me a picture
of Mary at the crib of Jesus—
She said the image of Mary
reminded her of one of my daughters

I framed the picture
and hung it on the wall
not because of any resemblance
to my daughter, but
because I was moved
by the striking look of anguish
upon Mary's lovely face

This had to have been the day
Mary and Joseph went to the temple
to dedicate Jesus, the day
they offered two turtledoves
as a sacrifice for their firstborn Son

Simeon was present when they came in
and knew immediately

by the power of the Holy Spirit
that this Child was
God's promised Savior

He told Mary:
A sword will pierce your soul!

This silent night in Bethlehem
as Jesus lay sleeping
Mary lifts his tiny hand
to her trembling lips
She wonders about God's marvelous plan
wonders how a Savior saves

and as she wonders, she feels
the point of an unseen sword
pressing against her flesh:

What did that wise old man mean?

There's so much I do not know—

So much I do not want to know

Tonight.

'TWAS THE NIGHT... OF ALL NIGHTS!
Matthew 2; Luke 2 NASB

Children, gather round. It's time for a story,
one that's filled with hallelujahs and glory.

It's about the glorious night of all nights,
angels and magi and sight of all sights!

About God, a virgin, the birth of a king,
wooly sheep, poor shepherds, and gift giving!

My story takes place long ago, far away
and starts with a Babe in a crib full of hay;

His mother's a virgin, His father is God,
the birth, a miraculous Heavenly nod.

The Baby is born in a Bethlehem barn
near a few smelly animals, like on a farm.

Poor shepherds in a field shudder with fright
when suddenly the dark sky fills up with light

as beautiful angels, bright splendors winging,
tell of the birth with hallelujahs and singing!

The Birth of Messiah

So, the shepherds and sheep the very next morn
set off to visit this special Newborn.

Rich wise men follow a bright beaming star
to the Bethlehem barn; the journey is far.

They ride astride camels, carrying treasures
to give to the One they'll worship forever.

Why in the world would they do such strange things?
Why travel so far? Why great treasures bring?

The reason is simple, the Babe in the hay
becomes the world's Savior, Who takes sin away.

His name is Jesus and He loves you and me
and wants us to love Him for eternity.

That was the night of all nights here on Earth…
the wonderful story of Jesus' birth!

CHAPTER TWO

THE DEATH OF MESSIAH

Like Mary, at the Feet of Jesus
John 11 1–46; John 12 1–8 NASB

Lord, I've come to curl up
close to Your sandals
like Mary of Bethany
my ears primed
to absorb each word You speak
I've tuned out concerns
that would pull me
from this footstool
and will not be bothered
by deeds or distractions
that would drown Your voice
If Martha insists
on doing busywork
she must do it alone
for nothing is more important to me
than sitting right here
right now, with You

And I will wail
at Your sacred feet
like Mary of Bethany
when my strength falters—
I shall wrap my quivering arms
around Your sturdy ankles

The Death of Messiah

allow my tears to run in rivulets
down Your dusty feet—
stir You to weep, too
till resurrection happens

But especially, Lord
I long to anoint Your precious feet
like Mary of Bethany
and come with all that I have
as she, bearing nard
for I, too, yearn to soothe
with pure, lavish fragrance
the calloused heels and soles
toes and arches
I, too, know well—
the very feet that carried Good News
to my ears and heart,
beautiful feet, bleeding feet
pierced through for me
I shall unpin my hair, humbly
like Mary of Bethany
take Your dust
as diamonds, upon me
I desire to be, unto you, Lord
a sweet aroma

and if I be scolded, as was she
by one who couldn't possibly understand
so be it...
so be it

AT CHORAZIN

Israel Pilgrimage (1986)
Matthew 11:21 NASB

We're at Chorazin, trying
to make ourselves comfortable
amid the ancient ruins
of the cursed city

I look for a patch
of dry grass to sit upon;
others sit on some rocks
Wayne props himself
against an acacia tree.

We're wearing head coverings
to shield us from the sun—
It's hot!

Beside us are box lunches
and water bottles
that we've brought
from the hotel
We open our Bibles
to Luke 10:13:

The Death of Messiah

Woe to you Chorazin!
Woe to you Bethsaida!

Wayne[2] begins teaching—

I think of Jesus—
imagine Him propped
against a tree
like Wayne

imagine myself at His feet—
like Mary of Bethany
like an apostle

imagine us opening
our lunch sacks—
barley loaves, some fish
fresh from the depths
of the Galilee nearby
imagine listening to every word
as the Master pronounces woes
on the unrepentant cities

That was nearly
two millennia ago—
This is 1986
It is Wayne who is explaining

---

[2] Rev. Wayne Monbleau is the founder of Loving Grace Ministries and host of the Christian radio call in counseling program, "Let's Talk About Jesus."

Behold the Lamb...poetically!

the Scriptures to us
not Jesus

We offer praise to God
and sing Hallels from the Psalms
A few birds are chirping
The sun-scorched clumps
of grass are lumpy beneath me
I smell the dry earth
and swat at a few pesky gnats
Perspiration beads up on my brow
I wipe it away
It is, I suppose, much the same
as it was way back then

and as it was then for them
I want the Word
to take root inside of me—
be it woes and chastisements
be it beatitudes and blessings—
take root
as it did in Mary
as it did in the apostles:

*for I, too, am a disciple
of the Lord*

SOMETIMES I WISH
A Prayer of Thanksgiving to My Savior

How can I tell
how can I show
how grateful I am
that You are my Savior?

Sometimes I wish
it were possible to
leave the roast in the oven
the suds in the sink

and follow my heart's cry
to the land of the Bible
to climb Calvary's hill
in beautiful Zion

Oh! If it were possible—

I'd fall to my knees
at the foot of the Cross
and wrap my arms tightly
'round its stained wooden base

and press a trembling cheek
against the old splintered grain
and thank You for Love
so wide and so deep
beyond what I can fathom

then I'd kiss it and weep
kiss it and weep

and whisper, *I love You*
from the depths of my being
for I'm eternally grateful
Jesus, My Lord

JESUS LAUGHED

Each of us has our own concept of Jesus—
As for me, I think He laughed a lot
Yes, I picture Jesus throwing his head back
with a wide winsome smile
and laughing heartily from the gut
and I think He did it often

I know it doesn't say so in Scripture
but still, I imagine the One
Who hung out with the twelve
shared some mighty amusing stories
around the campfire on starry summer evenings
I figure He even occasionally bore the brunt
of good natured razzing
and backslapping by the brethren
as they passed around roasted fish
and barley loaves on the shore of the Galilee

A guest at parties and weddings
Jesus was actually accused
of being a winebibber and glutton
He wouldn't have received
those kinds of invitations
and that kind of reputation
if He had been solemn and grim

And speaking of wine, I'm quite certain
no somber individual would have
turned H_2O into the fruit of the vine
so a wedding feast could proceed
with expected merrymaking and
no embarrassment for the host

Oh! I'm sure Jesus was great fun to be with—
that mothers readily handed babies to Him
that He kissed them, blessed them
chucked their chins and tickled their tummies
causing them to giggle and coo

I picture children climbing up on His lap
and being bounced on His knees
as He told stories about Jonah and Daniel
I'll bet He even tossed a leather ball
back and forth with the neighborhood lads
and when someone approached Him
with despair and grief and longing
my mind's eye sees Him
wrapping His loving arms around
the one in need—
turning sorrow into hope

Oh! It's true, Jesus got plenty stirred up
with righteous indignation—
even knocked over vendor tables
in the Temple courts

THE DEATH OF MESSIAH

and vented his anger vehemently
at hypocritical Pharisees

but this was the world His Father created
and loved so much
that He sent Him here
to save

Yes, I believe He laughed a lot
in spite of the fact
the dreaded Cross stood before Him
because He knew His mission
and of the joy to come

Indeed, the joy
for what He would accomplish *for us*
was already in Him

Yes, Jesus knew there was a time to laugh
and a time for anger
as well as a time to weep

Oh! I am touched by His humanity—

No wonder I love Him

MARY
Luke 1 and 2 and John 19:25–27 NASB

She was a real maiden
gracious and virtuous
so she trembled
as any girl might
at an angel's visit
But she had real faith
in a real God
and she said, *Yes.*

She was a real woman
not blue-gowned in plaster
A poor carpenter's wife
not an artist's rendering
gilded and haloed
She bulged big with child
as she rode astride an ass
and during her real travail
brought forth a baby
in a Bethlehem stable

She was a real mother
He was a real son
She nursed him

The Death of Messiah

changed him
bathed and cradled him
as any mother would
She smiled at his first word
saw him take his first step
and when he fell
and scraped his tender knees
she washed away blood
not yet deemed Precious
and soothed him
with soft lullabies

When he was twelve
and they discovered
he was missing
as they traveled home
after the Passover
she was anxious
as any mother would be
and heaved a great sigh
when they found him, safe
in the temple courts

Yes, she was a real mom
and he was a real son
so, it's not surprising
it was she
who sensed his power
she who encouraged him to act

Behold the Lamb...poetically!

at the wedding feast
when wine stopped flowing
for she knew
she just knew...

and she was real
at the Crossbeams
Simeon had told her
long, long ago
a sword would pierce her
Though hers be bloodless
it penetrated sharp
and deep, as truly
as the gaping wounds
she now was powerless
to soothe

He looked down
from His agony
into hers—
gave her to mother
his friend
gave his friend
to be her son

It was always about love

She was a real mom
He is the real Savior

IMAGINE

Imagine worshipping a cooing one moment, whimpering the next, born to save us, sweet baby God, lying in a trough filled with scratchy straw, needing a diaper change.

Imagine worshipping a stone-kicking, frog-in-pocket, sticky-fingered, tousle-haired God, gleefully splish-splashing through mud puddles along a rocky Nazareth road.

Imagine worshipping a nose-in-the-Scroll, confident little boy God, teaching in the Temple, confounding elders with astonishing Truths, as His parents search for Him.

Imagine worshipping a rugged, long-haired, son-of-a-carpenter adolescent God, as He learns (ironically) to skillfully select woods and deftly wield a hammer and nails.

Imagine worshipping a gregarious, life-of-the-party, wedding guest God, Who miraculously turns stone jars of purification water into jars of finest wine at Cana.

Imagine worshipping a child-embracing, woe-pronouncing, multitude-feeding, leper-cleansing God, Who walks upon water, instructs the wind, and even raises the dead.

Imagine worshipping a bread-breaking, wine-offering, foot-washing God, Who soon to be betrayed, beseeches His Heavenly Father, and sweats blood in an olive garden.

Imagine worshipping a thirty-something, blood-splattered, fist-struck, scourged and spat-upon God, laboriously lugging a cumbersome crossbeam to His own execution.

Imagine worshipping a thorn-crowned, sword-pierced, crucified-with-common-criminals sacrificial Lamb of God, as He dies *sinless* for the sin of the world.

Imagine worshipping a resurrected three-days-after-burial God, Who appears ALIVE! Yes, ALIVE! in His own burial garden, in locked rooms and to strangers along the road.

Imagine worshipping this crucified, resurrected, gloriously ascending-in-the-clouds, victorious Son of God, Who says, *Go into the world and tell them*. Tell them...

He did it for them.

Imagine.

Ash Wednesday Reflection

It's Ash Wednesday—

Off in the distance I hear thunder
thunder, like the sound of a big bass drum

There's a BOOM and a BOOM and a BOOM
and a BOOM

like ticking and ticking and ticking
of a clock. Like a pulse pulsing
Like beats. Heartbeats

Mine—

I'm reminded of time wasted
and time used wisely
of goals realized
and goals not met

Have I said the important things?
Have I done them?
Have I given enough?
Have I loved enough? Forgiven?
Accepted forgiveness?

Is the world better because I'm here?

Behold the Lamb...poetically!

Have I done what I need to do with God?

I listen for the next strike to the drum
and the next

BOOM and a BOOM and a BOOM

I don't want the rhythm to stop

but it will

I recall our vigil at Joanne's bedside—
Remember holding my breath, waiting for her next
waiting for each heartbeat. Wishing
my hoping was enough
to keep her
The beat goes on. It won't falter

until BOOM and a BOOM... BOOM
and silence

dead silence

and that's it

That's when what I've done
or haven't done

with God

takes over

Acceptance

I accept this bitter cup
filled to the brim
with the wine
of sorrow
I'll take
and drink
it dry

For I have tasted
the sweet wine
of the red
grapes
of joy
the wine
of gladness
the wine
of blessing

I accept this cross—

I will lug its weight
upon my
bony shoulder
and trudge
the pathway

of travail
When
I misstep
and stumble
I'll call for help

My cross
is so, so small
compared to Yours
My bitter cup
sweet honey
All I need
to make it

Jesus

is Your hand
and Your deep
unfathomable
Love…

I'M NOT JEWISH

Romans 11; Romans 2:28–29; John 19:37 NASB

except that the sap
which rises
from sturdy old olive roots
flows through the veins
of this grafted branch

I'm not Jewish
except for my flesh
which still shudders
at the Shoah
(of sisters and brothers
of the natural branch)
and the same root
and swears
I'd have done something...
Something

I'm not Jewish
except for my feet
which have walked
the holy, well-worn pathways
in Eretz Yisrael[3]

---

[3] Eretz Yisrael is Hebrew for land of Israel.

Behold the Lamb...Poetically!

except for my fingertips
which pressed petitions
between stones
of the Western Wall

except for my ears
which perk to the cantor's
chanting of the Shema
the Aaronic Benediction
the Kiddush
over bread and wine

except for my eyes
which look
upon the Lamb,
my Atonement

except for my lips
which chant
ancient baruchas[4]
to HaShem[5]

I'm not Jewish
except for my heart
which bears the cloven mark
of circumcision

---

[4] Baruch is the Hebrew word for blessed.

[5] HaShem is the literal Hebrew translation for The Name (Adonai).

The Death of Messiah

and loves Yeshua,
the Jewish Messiah
Who was pierced
for my transgressions
Who shed
His precious Jewish Blood
for me

As the Fall Holidays Approach
Leviticus 23 NASB

I reach for my sweater against the chill
The crickets are chittering
Sunflowers have shed their golden petals
and a few green tomatoes remain
abandoned on the vines
It's September—
the High Holy Days are approaching

Soon I will gather with mishpocheh[6]
in the parking lot outside Beth Israel
We will observe Rosh Hoshanna
Rabbi Jonathan will sound
his kudu shofar beneath the full moon—
Tekiah—Shevarim—Teruah—Tekiah Gedolah[7]

Sages tell us the first day of the month of Tishri
is the day God created the world
the world He so loved
the world He gave His only Son to save
The trumpeting reminds me

---

[6] Mishpocheh is the Hebrew word for family.

[7] These are names of sounds the shofar (ram's horn) makes on Rosh Hoshanna.

to reflect upon my relationship
with this God of my salvation
reminds me, humbly, to prepare for Yom Kippur

So I ponder the Day of Atonement
ponder the High Priest entering the Holy of Holies
sprinkling the blood of the sacrifice
upon the Mercy Seat
ponder the sacrificed goat and the scapegoat
ponder forgiveness
ponder my sins, atoned for by Yeshua[8]
ponder my High Priest, the Perfect Sacrifice
Who offered His Very Own Blood
on my behalf

Next will be Sukkot
the Feast of Tabernacles—
From inside a leafy sukkah
I'll be reminded of the sojourn of God's people
to the Promised Land
reminded of my very own sojourn
toward God's promise—
eternal life with Him
in Heaven

---

[8] Yeshua is the name of Jesus in Hebrew.

THE PASSOVER LAMB
Exodus 12 NASB

Abba went into the sheepfold to choose a spotless lamb,
as Moses gave instructions that he got from the I AM.

Our lamb, indeed, was spotless, so I named him Wooly Bright;
we brought him inside to live with us, morning, noon, and night.

I ran my fingers through his coat and fed him from my hand;
I put fresh water in his trough; he's the best lamb in the land!

Today he'll be our sacrifice. Moses said this must be done.
He must die that I may live, for I'm a firstborn son.

We've been oppressed by slavery; Pharaoh will not let us go,
but God's mighty arm will save us. We'll watch His power flow.

Moses told us, take lamb's blood and brush it on the lintel
then we will be protected; it almost sounds too simple.

Tonight we will leave Egypt and journey far from home,
but I'll remember Wooly Bright wherever I may roam.

The Death of Messiah

Someday the world will see in this, God's salvation plan;
God's Son will be the sacrifice, the great Passover Lamb!

For as God will use blood of lambs to set His people free,
the precious Blood of Jesus will save sinners... you and me.

THE NAME

YHVH
the tetragrammaton
the unutterable
four consonants
of the Most Holy Name
of the Great I AM
Who was, Who is
Who is to come

Whose radiant Face
eyes of mortals
could not behold
and live

Whose Holy Ark
mere mortals
could not touch
and live

until He
Who always was
came in the Person
of His Son

and mortals flocked
to hear Him speak

The Death of Messiah

children climbed
upon His lap
sick and lowly
sought His touch
even grasped
at His hem

By His Word
even the dead arose

When He
Who always was
shed His *innocent* Blood
upon Calvary's Cross
the thick woven veil
to the Holy of Holies
tore top to bottom
that *all* may enter in

By His Holy Name
Salvation comes

Now we know Him
as our Brother
Savior, Friend

We call Him
Jesus/Yeshua

the Messiah

THE LAMB

Exodus 12; John 19 NASB
Revelation 5: 12–13 NIV

O look upon the innocent
the unblemished lamb, slain at twilight
as God decreed through Moses
See its blood upon the doorposts, upon the lintel
The Israelites consume it along with bitter herbs
reminiscent of affliction
They eat hurriedly, prepared for departure
loins girded, sandals on their feet
staff in hand, the lamb within
Look upon the foreshadows
see their hazy shapes coming into focus—
It's the Passover of the Lord

God struck His mighty hand against Egypt
and the firstborn of man and livestock were slain
As God looked upon the lamb's blood
on the doorposts, on the lintels
He passed over the Israelite dwellings
and delivered His chosen, saved
by the blood of the Lamb
Look upon the foreshadows
see their hazy shapes coming into focus—
It's the Passover, the Holy Passover of the Lord

THE DEATH OF MESSIAH

O look upon the Innocent, the Unblemished One
the Lamb upon the Cross
slain in unison with other lambs at Passover
See the crimson Blood trickling down
the thorn-crowned Face
streaming from His hands and feet
See the iron spikes, the gaping stripes
the Suffering Servant
Oh! Gaze into the Eyes of the Lamb
the Atonement for all sin
It's the Passion, the Holy Passion of the Lord

The Redemptive Lambs
meet in the foreshadows
Their shapes come into focus—
They are One

The precious Blood
of the Lamb upon the Cross
redeems the world—

We are saved
by the Blood of the Lamb—

It is finished. *Alleluia!*

O look upon the glorious One
the Lamb standing as if slain
Hear the multitudes proclaim—

Behold the Lamb...Poetically!

*Worthy is the Lamb Who was slain
to receive power and wealth
and wisdom and strength
and honor and glory and praise!*

*... To Him who sits on the throne
and to the Lamb, be praise and honor
and glory and power for ever and ever!*

Amen

About "The Lamb"

I began writing inspirational poetry, seriously, in the late 1980s. I read, studied, and experimented with writing styles, trying to find my voice.

Shortly after marrying Leo Carolan, in 1991, I was sitting at my desk in work at Kearfott in Wayne, NJ, one Friday afternoon, when a vision of a Lamb upon a cross momentarily flashed before my eyes. Strangely, it was a cocoa-colored lamb. Its sad dark eyes looked down and penetrated me. I knew at that moment I would write a poem about the Lamb upon a cross.

That evening, Leo and I went to the Shabbat service at Beth Israel Messianic Center, then in Garfield, NJ. I began talking with a woman I knew named Elaine. I complimented her on a piece of unique jewelry she was wearing. It was a gold Star of David with a realistic platinum lamb affixed over it. She wore it on a chain around her neck. Elaine explained to me that she had the piece custom made. The Star had a wood grain design, which represented the cross to her. There it was, for the second time that day, the Lamb upon a cross. I immediately knew the poem swirling in my mind would begin with the lambs in Exodus that were slain before the Passover.

Behold the Lamb...Poetically!

Writing the poem was particularly significant because I felt God's hand strongly upon me as I wrote. When the draft was finished, I prepared to show it to Leo to get his opinion. Because this poem was deeply personal and important, I prayed first and asked God to give me the grace to accept any criticism Leo might offer without becoming sensitive or defensive. He asked me to read the poem to him. As I read aloud, there was one word I suddenly realized needed to be changed. I waited for Leo's input. He said he liked it a lot, but there was just one word he recommended I change. Of course, it was the very same word. Praise the Lord for the amazing grace He gives. I consider this to be my miracle poem.

LOVE AND THE AKEDAH
THE BINDING OF ISAAC
Genesis 22; John 19 NIV

Take your son
your only son
whom you love…

Twenty-two chapters into Scripture
and it's the first time love is mentioned
as God tells Abraham:

Sacrifice Isaac
as a burnt offering

What swirls
through the mind
of this old patriarch
(who after a hundred years
fathers the son
of God's promise…
the son he loves
and proudly watches grow)
What swirls as he swings
the sharp axe, splitting wood

It was a three-day journey
from Beersheba to Moriah—
Leaving his servants behind
Abraham hands Isaac
the bundled wood
and carries fire and knife
up the mount
himself

Avi (my father),
where is the lamb?

God will provide the lamb
my son

Abraham erects an altar of stone
arranges the wood and binds the lad
(whose faith and obedience
must be at least as great as his own)

Unflinching before the God
he has finally come to trust
the aged patriarch
(known to lie
to save his own skin
known to try to pull off
God's covenant himself
when it seemed God was slow
in keeping His promise)

The Death of Messiah

this same patriarch...
raises the glinting blade
above his son, his only son
whom he loves...

Split second
to knife-fall
the angel of the Lord calls out:

Abraham! Abraham!
Do not lay a hand on the boy...

The old man
who has proven he would
withhold nothing from his God—
drops the bloodless blade
unbinds and embraces Isaac

and there, tangled
in a thicket, struggles
the substitute sacrifice
... a ram

Two millennia later
God's Son
His only Son
Whom He loves
carries wood
of a crossbeam
up the very same mountain

BEHOLD THE LAMB...POETICALLY!

No angel of the Lord
arrives last moment
to halt the hammer fall
No ram appears
in a thicket

For God so loves
the world
He provides...

His Son
His only Son... *the Sacrificial Lamb*

A Poem for Lent

I scan *Google Images*
looking for a depiction of the Crucifixion
to illustrate a Lenten poem on my blog
I'm unable to look squarely at the pictures—
Many are so heart-wrenching, so horrific
I have to turn away

I certainly realize how gruesome
Jesus' crucifixion was—
Doesn't everyone?
We have heard the account
so many times
that its image is seared vividly
upon our hearts and minds

The four Gospels
provide matter-of-fact statements
to state that Jesus was crucified
sparing us the details
of His suffering

Oh, I'm well aware
it is 2000 years later
and no holds are barred
when it comes to portrayals of violence

I go to the movies
I watch TV

I've squirmed through
The Passion of the Christ[9]
with my heart beating fast
and eyes tightly closed
during the bloodiest sequences
I've read *A Doctor at Calvary*[10]
in which each and every stain
on the Shroud of Turin
is elaborated upon
in minute medical detail

I do not need
more graphic words and pictures
My mind's eye sees
His thorn-crowned Head
His nail-pierced hands
My mind's ear hears

Father, forgive them…

… why hast Thou forsaken Me?

---

[9] *The Passion of the Christ* is a 2004 American biblical drama film directed by Mel Gibson and written by Gibson and Benedict Fitzgerald. The film primarily covers the final twelve hours of Jesus' life.

[10] *A Doctor at Calvary* by Pierre Barbet, MD, published by Image Books, a division of Doubleday & Co., Inc., Garden City, NY

The Death of Messiah

It is finished.

My mind's heart
feels His agony

At last, I click on an image—
a crossbeam, a circle of thorns
and three nails

I post it on the blog
insert my poem

and shudder
a most grateful shudder
that my beloved Savior
endured that terrible Cross
for me

THE SCRAPBOOK GRANDMA MADE FOR ME

I picked up my grandchildren
at Saint Mary's elementary school
They tossed their heavy backpacks
into the back of the car
got in and fastened their seatbelts
They know the routine—
don't need to be reminded anymore

As we drove off
I could hear them in the back seat
talking about Lent and fasting
Dean and Alana gave up electronics
Their big brother Logan
now in high school
gave up chocolate
Dean asked, *Grandma
what did you give up?*

I told Dean I didn't give up
anything this Lent, instead
I give Jesus a gift of new poems—
Some days I spend quiet time
writing poems that give glory to Him
and every day I post
a Lenten poem on my blog

The Death of Messiah

Dean said, *Wow! That's a lot
of poems, Grandma!*

I explained that it's perfectly fine
to give up things for forty days, but
sometimes people do other things
like donating to a charity
or visiting the sick
or baking cookies for an elderly neighbor
anything that draws them closer to God

Then I thought about my own grandmother—
She lived next door
when I was growing up
Grandma loved the Lord
and often talked to me about Him
She even made a special scrapbook
with a cardboard cover for me
that she decorated with flowers
carefully cut from a Burpee seed catalog
The scrapbook contained pictures of children
kittens and puppies, and *Howdy Doody*
but more importantly, it contained
the eleven-chapter story by Charles Dickens
that he wrote for his children in the 1840s
called, *The Life of Our Lord*
The story was published as a serial
in the Paterson Morning Call, in the 1950s

Behold the Lamb...poetically!

I still have that scrapbook
still appreciate that Grandma took the time
to make it just for me

It's the kind of thing grandmas do—
Important things like that

ACCUSTOMED TO THE CROSS

I'm accustomed to the Cross.

I've seen it since childhood
gleaming high atop steeples,
crucifixes behind altar rails,
on hospital walls,
on bedroom walls,
depicted in framed masterpieces,
depicted in sculpted masterpieces,
described in written masterpieces,
marking graves in cemeteries,
illustrated in holy books,
affixed to lapels,
tattooed on forearms,
hanging silver and golden
and studded with diamonds
and sapphires from the necks
of men, women, children—
hanging, hanging on my mind.

So accustomed, yet
sometimes it is everywhere
and I don't see it at all.

Behold the Lamb...Poetically!

Today I see it afresh
sturdy and wooden and terrifying
through Good Friday eyes
that sends streams down my cheeks
as blood streams from His wounds.
I shudder,
mindful of the Man
dying upon the beams
and the reason He is there—

Shudder
at the horror of it, Jesus my Lamb,
at the magnitude of it, Jesus my King,
at the love upon it, Jesus my Friend,
and my gratitude for it,
O Blessed Jesus,
my precious Lord and Savior
Who by Death
and Resurrection
purchased eternal life... *for me*.

PACES OF A LAMB

He was led like a lamb to the slaughter,
and as a sheep before her shearers is silent,
so he did not open his mouth.

(ISAIAH 53:7 N.I.V.)

Father Bob drained the cup
and replaced the cover
on the brass pyx of Hosts.
Communion over
the two old friends
settled back
in their kitchen chairs

A natural storyteller
Leo began to reminisce
about Mr. Sattel
his neighbor in Roselle Park
in the 1940s—
the best bologna maker
at the pork store nearby

Eventually the neighbor
purchased some farmland
and moved to Penns Grove
where he built a slaughterhouse

Behold the Lamb...Poetically!

Leo spent time there
the summer between grammar
and high school

He had watched Mr. Sattel subdue
fat squealing hogs
and tenacious bulls
Saw him and his helpers
pull resisting livestock
by a rope fed through a nose ring
to another ring in the floor
where struggling animals
were systematically
slaughtered
one at a time

Mr. Sattel grew hardened
even provoked to anger
by the tugging and digging in of hooves
amid the ominous odor of blood
which roused the desperate instinct
against death—

The grueling labor of slaughter
left him no energy for grief

but his steel eyes glazed over
one muggy afternoon
when he told Leo:

The Death of Messiah

I did a lamb once.

It walked right alongside me
up the ramp.

I'll never
do it
again.

An edgy silence followed—
silent as paces of a lamb

There they sat, two white-haired friends
washed by the shed blood
of One Docile Lamb
Who walked Calvary's ramp

two thousand years ago

BETWEEN THE PALMS AND THE CROSS
Matthew 21:1–11 and 27:11–26 NASB

I'm sitting here meditating
upon that final week
wondering what happened to His followers
after Jesus entered Jerusalem
riding astride a donkey
as people spread their coats before Him
along the dusty road
Wondering about those followers
the ones who cut branches from palm trees
and waved them at Him in homage, proclaiming:

Hosanna to the Son of David!
Hosanna in the highest!

After all, He was their humble King

I'm sitting here wondering what happened
between then and days later
when Jesus stood before Pilate
amid a crowd of onlookers
persuasive chief priests and elders
and everyone began shouting:

The Death of Messiah

Crucify Him! Crucify Him!

Did they forget the taste of water
that He turned into wine?

Did they forget the healed lepers and the blind?

Did they forget Him preaching
to the multitudes, *Blessed be the poor...*
and the thousands He fed with a few loaves and fish

Did they forget He healed a pitiful demoniac
and the woman with an issue of blood

Could they have forgotten that he said to the dead girl,
Talitha kum, and she sprang right up and walked

And Lazarus? Could they possibly have forgotten
that Jesus called His friend out of the tomb
and Lazarus emerged, grave clothes coiled
around his body... *after three days!*

I'm still sitting here wondering about
how quickly they turned
from their hosannas
to calling for His death

Wasn't there one clear-headed believer
one unable-to-be-swayed witness

BEHOLD THE LAMB...POETICALLY!

one unshakable faithful-unto-death follower
to boldly shout out in protest...

No!

No. There wasn't

Not even one

COMMEMORATING THE LAST SUPPER
Israel Pilgrimage (2006)
John 13; Matthew 26:26–29; Acts 2:1–13 NASB

We realize this is not the actual place
where Messiah celebrated
the Passover with His disciples
on the night before He suffered
not the very place
where He took bread and broke it
took the cup and shared it
not the room in which He said:

Do this in remembrance of Me

but here we are in the Land
here we are in the relative vicinity
We know the actual Upper Room is long gone
but this is a room and it's upstairs
as near as we can possibly get
besides, in the spirit
we are here, transported
so this is plenty good enough
We break into praise and worship
to celebrate the Passover meal
the taking of the towel

the washing of feet
the reclining at the table
the dipping of the bread
the very first communion
and another noteworthy occasion—
Pentecost

The presence of the Spirit
falls so mightily upon us
we expect blazing tongues of fire
to tumble down from Heaven
and alight upon our heads

BETTER FOR HIM HAD HE NOT BEEN BORN

*...But woe to that man who betrays the Son of Man!
It would be better for him if he had not been born.*
                              (MATT 26:24B (NIV))

He controlled the money bag
dipped into the money bag
dipped with Jesus at table
mingled with Him
chewed the fat
as they roasted fish
along the shore of the Galilee

Judas watched Him heal
the blind and lame
even raise the dead
was there when He fed
hungry multitudes
calmed a raging squall
and walked billow to billow
upon the storm-tossed sea

He heard Him teach
beatitudes, parables
even how to pray
observed His tenderness

as children climbed
upon His lap
observed His mercy
to those who sinned much

The day Mary anointed Jesus' feet
with extravagant nard
and dried them
with her unpinned hair
it was he who complained
the perfume should have been sold
the money given to the poor—
yes, it was he, holder
of the purse strings

When this same apostle agreed
to betray his master
for a handful of silver
did he think
the Miracle Worker
would somehow slip away
unscathed, as He had
the day He was driven
out of the synagogue
by an angry mob
intent on throwing Him
off a cliff

The Death of Messiah

Woe to the mercenary
betrayer of the Son of Man
... Mammon had always been
his greater god

Their final evening
at the Paschal meal
the Master stooped
to wash filth
from His betrayer's feet

Judas partook of the Bread
drank of the Wine
and when Jesus dipped a morsel
and gave it to him
from His very own hand
the taker took that, too

Later, in the garden
following Jesus' great travail
Judas approached Him
with armed cohorts
called Him, *Rabbi*
kissed his face
still damp with blood and sweat
as the Rabbi called him, *Friend*

The word echoed
echoed, echoed

Behold the Lamb...poetically!

in thunderous
heartbeats
till he flung
the tarnished coins
through temple doors
till he tied
a ragged noose around his neck
and hanged his wretched self
from a jutting twisted limb

At the Garden of Gethsemane
Israel Pilgrimage (2006)

We are given a little time to stroll
through a grove of olive trees—
the Garden of Gethsemane

Gethsemane means olive press
I am a living olive press
I walk along the path
trampling ripened fruit
beneath my feet

The ancient trees
which sometimes live
more than 4,000 years
have taken on characteristics
of crippled old men
Sinewy twisted limbs
are gnarled and pocked
The bark is jagged and gray

A few ripe black olives remain
dangling from branches
like little ebony orbs

As I meander, I wonder
about my Savior
and the night before
He was crucified
The night He prayed
among trees such as these
the night He asked His Father
if the cup could be removed

Surely, the crushing weight
of the olive press
bore heavily upon His shoulders
as He offered prayer so deep
so utterly wrenching
the intensity of its passion
caused His Body
to sweat blood from His pores
Oh, my Jesus!

I shudder—
We come together
for an anointing service
Rabbi Jonathan asks
what we would like
to be anointed for
He touches each forehead
with fragrant oil
and prays

The Death of Messiah

I ask for words
to give glory to the Lord
in my poems

Bob asks to draw closer to God
and adds his desire
that the Lord will always be
at the center of our marriage—

Oh, sweet bridegroom
thank you for your heartfelt
honeymoon prayer

THE DUNGEON

Israel Pilgrimage (2006)
Matthew 26: 69–75 NASB

There is a pit
beneath the House of Caiaphas
a once dark, dismal, terrifying hole
into which prisoners
were lowered by ropes
under their armpits

Our Lord Jesus likely
was brought here directly
from the Garden of Gethsemane
on the night He was betrayed by Judas

The scene seems less horrifying today
than when I was here in 1986
Then, it was easier to imagine
a terrifying incarceration
of a prisoner, especially
an innocent prisoner, alone
amid ominous dampness and vermin
in the very bowels of the earth

THE DEATH OF MESSIAH

The pit is located beneath a church—
The Church of Saint Peter of Gallicantu
(of the cock's crow)
named for where in the courtyard
Peter denied knowing Jesus three times

It's been spiffed up—
It's brighter. The descent, easier
It's not nearly as dismal and ominous

but, back in eighty-six
as Wayne Monbleau[11] read Psalm 22
in that detestable dungeon:

… they pierced
my hands and my feet.
I can count all my bones….[12]

I closed my eyes and literally
trembled… trembled… trembled
imagining how terribly Jesus suffered
to wash my sins away

---

[11] Rev. Wayne Monbleau is the founder of Loving Grace Ministries and host of the Christian call in counseling radio program, "Let's Talk About Jesus."

[12] Psalm 22:17–18 NASB

PILATE'S IRONY
Matthew 27:11–26 NASB

During my first pilgrimage to Israel
archeologist and guide, Micha Ashkenazi
took us to Caesarea to view a replica
of a piece of limestone
partially inscribed with the name *Pontius Pilatus*

Micha had been a member of the team
that unearthed the stone
during a dig there, in 1961

It is the only evidence
of the historical existence
of the Roman governor
outside the New Testament
and writings of Josephus Flavius

Interesting, Pilate, who may have given
a modicum of credence to his wife's warning
to have nothing to do with Jesus
did make an abysmal effort
to prevent the crucifixion
by setting Barabbas
before the riled multitude

THE DEATH OF MESSIAH

When the crowd shouted to free Barabbas
and called for death to Jesus
their chants of

Crucify Him! Crucify Him!

drummed in his ears

Pilate asked for a basin of water
He washed his hands in front of them—
as if water could possibly cleanse him
of responsibility for what would happen next

The irony is that even now
thousands of years hence
contempt for this man is as clear
as his name etched in stone—

for wherever believers gather
and proclaim their creed

Jesus…

*suffered under Pontius Pilate
was crucified, dead, and buried…*

Pilate's guilt is an indelible stain
that can never be
washed from our minds

REMEMBERING GOOD FRIDAYS

*In memory of my paternal grandmother,
Maude Ann Walsh*

When I was a young girl, back in the 1950s
my grandmother said
there should be no talking on Good Friday
between the hours of one and three

no running around, no radio, and no TV
all out of respect for our Savior
Who suffered and died
upon the Cross at Calvary

so try though I did to be silent and still
I was as fidgety, squirmy, and irksome
as any healthy active kid would be
who had not yet grasped
the profound depth of what happened
that terrible good day when Jesus died

and in the 1970s when my own children
were young and restless
I brought them to church
during the very same hours Grandma decreed
to venerate the holy Cross

The Death of Messiah

We'd approach the altar
where the Crucifix was displayed
kneel down and kiss the nail-pierced feet of Jesus
or solemnly watch a reenactment of the Passion
by the youth group

Now, so many years later
now that I am a grandmother myself
I sit without fidgeting and fumbling
willingly turn off the radio and the TV
and carve out meaningful time to meditate
upon all my precious Lord endured
to save me from my sins

Sometimes I sing
"Were You There When They Crucified My Lord?"
Sometimes I weep
and sometimes, like today, I write a poem

Always, Jesus' great sacrifice breaks my heart
and always, looking back
at that astonishing empty tomb
I'm reminded of the Hallelujah Hope
I have in Him—*which is eternal*

Grandma would be so pleased

THE BLACK BRONCO
Good Friday, 2002

Discontented
sad, somewhat guilty...
Usually I'd have found time
in the afternoon
to sit meditatively
and ponder the significance
of this day
Sometimes I wrote poems
or sat quietly in a church
I might have listened
to a radio preacher
or just sung, soulfully
about the house
that old, haunting hymn chorus—

O sometimes it causes me
to tremble... tremble... tremble[13]

Eased into the day, holy
with a long, tepid bath

---

[13] "Were You There" was likely composed by African-American slaves in the nineteenth century. It was first published in William Eleazar Barton's 1899 *Old Plantation Hymns*.

THE DEATH OF MESSIAH

and a little book
about six miracles of Calvary—
Began contemplating the darkness
that fell upon the land
for three hours

but after that
the cares of this world
sent me scurrying helter-skelter
scrubbing the kitchen floor
returning curtains to JC Penney
grocery shopping for Easter dinner
Any meaningful reflections faded
in my slide from Mary to Martha

Returning from an errand edgy
I was stopped at a light
on Union Boulevard
Don't know what kind of a car
was in front of me
but in front of that car
was a black Bronco

On back of the Bronco
black on black was
the Crucifixion
Jesus, dying
in utter darkness
His head bent

shoulders thrust forward
like so many paintings I've seen

What was this?

After a moment, I realized
it was merely a reflection—
a silhouette cast by the shadow
of a telephone pole
and street lamp...
But it seemed real

I looked at the clock
It was 2:45

I drive up and down
Union Boulevard
day after day
year after year
but it was this day
this hour
this moment of need
He chose
to show me
yet again
all He did

for me

BLOOD SKY
GOOD FRIDAY 2014, PACKANACK LAKE, NEW JERSEY

I will display wonders in the sky and on the earth, blood, fire and columns of smoke. The sun will be turned into darkness and the moon into blood before the great and awesome day of the Lord comes.

(JOEL 2:30–31 NASB)

The alarm went off at 3:00 am, Tuesday
We went outdoors to gaze at the sky
hoping to get a glimpse
of the first blood moon of the tetrad—
Passover, 2014

It was there, but we couldn't see it
Dense clouds obscured our view

Blood moon or not, this week is crimson—
I've been thinking about blood in the Nile
blood on the lintels
death of the firstborn sons

I bought blood oranges in Fairway, yesterday
Had one for breakfast. It was sweet

BEHOLD THE LAMB...POETICALLY!

Today is Good Friday—
I am meditating upon the atonement
the Cross, the death of my Savior

Now it's evening—
I'm on my way to the Good Friday service
at the Jerusalem Center in Wayne
As I drive down Osborne Terrace
approaching Packanack Lake
the sky is incredible—amazing—red as blood
fiery red, red like I've never seen it before

As the setting sun shines on the still water
the lake mirrors the brilliant crimson firmament
and I can't help thinking of old Moses
as he dipped his staff into the Nile River

At the Jerusalem Center, the dancers
fittingly extol the Lamb Who was slain, and
Rabbi Jonathan speaks of the sun
setting and rising—
endings and beginnings

and I feel God may be telling me something, or
am I so deeply aware of Him this holy week
that I see Him everywhere
and in every blessed thing

It Pleased the Lord to Crush Him[14]

When I applied stinging iodine
to the tender knees of my children
or a corrective spank
or a hug to assuage a broken heart
I remember that
their wounds, hurts
even the chastisements
probably wounded me more than them—
Why, I would've become a she-lion
poised to pounce and mangle
bruisers of my own—
yet the very God I know as Love
was pleased to crush
was delighted to bruise[15]
His Very Own

So, *I shudder*, convinced
God's ways are infinitely higher
than my finite mind can grasp—
for God stayed His almighty hand
held His almighty tongue
waited it out in His Heaven

---

[14] Isaiah 53:10 "New American Standard Bible"

[15] Isaiah 53:10 , "Young's Literal Translation of the Holy Bible"

pleased, *even delighted*
to give His Only Son
innocent, docile as a lamb
to be mocked, bruised, spat upon
crowned with thorn branches
stripped and nailed naked to a tree—

yes, pleased and delighted was He
as the Most Precious Blood
of His Only Son
rained like rubies
upon the ground

Pleased and delighted *am I*
that the God Who so loves
crushed and bruised
His Very Own
for me

FATHER, FORGIVE THEM
Luke 23:34 NASB

It's Good Friday
and I'm doing what I usually do—
meditating on the Cross
and then writing a poem

Today I am thinking about forgiveness
and unforgiveness
thinking one of the things
that makes me marvel about Jesus
is that He looked down
upon the very men who mocked Him
the ones who scourged Him
who spat in His innocent face
then crowned Him with a twisted ring of thorns
and drove nails through His hands and feet

Yes, He looked at them
with unfathomable mercy
in His unspeakable agony
and implored His Father:
… forgive them
for they do not know what they are doing

Then I think of myself
of injustices done to me

Behold the Lamb...Poetically!

by people I've loved
people I've tried to forgive
and have forgiven
then taken back my forgiveness
over and over and over again
I've mulled over life's unfairness
replayed injustices, feeling righteous
feeling justified

then I am reminded (like today)
that *all* have sinned
so I let go and forgive again
and really want to
for God has forgiven me
so who am I
to remember puny injustices
against myself

Today, Jesus, as I meditate upon Your love
and the magnitude of Your sacrifice
my old wounds are infinitesimal
I don't want to harbor them
anymore

I'm asking for Your help
this Good Friday afternoon

Help me let it all go—

forever

HE REFUSED
Matthew 27:34 NASB

They mocked
and struck and spat and stripped
and drove spikes
through His hands and feet.
One offered wine and myrrh
to take the pointed edge
off the Excruciation.

The Savior
peered down
through kind, hot eyes,
pursed His parched lips
and shook His bleeding head.

He chose... *chose!*
to bear the fullness
of the sin
that nailed Him
to those crude
crossed beams,
chose to drink
the brimming chalice dry,

chose to pay the full price,
without bargain or barter,
without wholesaling
or discounting
or quibbling
or niggling it
of its terrible,
priceless
Value.

THE HEART-WRENCHING CRY
Matthew 27:46 NASB

Oh, I am sure God heard it
as He sat with His head in His hands
on the edge of His great golden throne
moments away from Victory

This wasn't the cry of physical pain
from crucifixion nails
pressing against Jesus' pierced flesh

No, this was different—
This was the cry of... Abba, where are You?
the utterance that shot from Earth to Heaven
from the One He was One with
from all eternity—

Why hast Thou forsaken Me?

This was the wuthering wail
from despair's deepest depth
as sin of all the world fell upon
the One who had never sinned

Behold the Lamb...Poetically!

This echoed as Satan snarled
his final snarl before
Atonement's Victorious Hallelujah!

and the Blood-washed expiation
of my sin and yours
of all sin past and present
sin of those yet unborn
those not yet conceived
sin of those who would not be born
for centuries and millenniums

This was the heart-wrenching cry before

It is finished!

the nod
of Jesus' thorn-crowned head

and His Father's most solemn

Amen!

in Glory

THE PIETA
Luke 2:25–35

After the earthquake
the peals of thunder
the flashes of lightning across the sky
After the curious crowds dispersed
Mary sat in ominous dimness
upon a mound of earth
at the base of the Cross
clutching the body
of her Son

She cradled Him
in the hollow of her lap
close to her bosom
as she had
when he was
her baby boy

Mary removed
thorns of mockery
that encircled His forehead
and tossed it to the side
Straining to see through her tears
she carefully picked

fragments of thorn needles
still stuck in His lifeless flesh
although they couldn't hurt Him
any longer

With her fingertips
she tenderly closed the lids
over His dark, vacant eyes
and smoothed
the disheveled, matted hair
... then she kissed Him

O, my beautiful Son...

Tears flowed
down her face onto His cheeks
mingling with dried blood
With the edge of her garment
she wiped some blood away

John came
and rested his hand
upon her trembling shoulder
He was now her son
She was now his mother

Mysteries
too deep to comprehend
swirled in her mind

The Death of Messiah

like the flap and flutter
of wings and overshadowing
Son of the Most High
and David's throne

like pregnant Elizabeth's joy
when the baby leapt in her womb
and the Baptizer himself, when grown
proclaiming his younger cousin
The Lamb of God, Who
takes away the sin of the world

and Simeon's prophesy
that Jesus would be
a Light of revelation
to the Gentiles and the glory
of the people of Israel

Where is the Light?
Where is the glory?
Where is the throne?

Overwhelmed by sorrow
so intense it stabbed her
deep, deep in her inner parts
Mary cried out in anguish
and rent her robe:

Behold the Lamb...Poetically!

*Was this what old Simeon meant
long ago in the Temple
when he held Jesus in his arms
and said a sword would pierce
my very soul?*

O my Son, my beautiful Son...

*I cannot fathom the ways of God, but
I do know this cannot be the end*

His Little Lamb

The Shepherd loves you, little lamb
He holds you to His breast
He strokes His hand along your back
with utmost tenderness

The hand He runs along your back
is scarred from long ago—
A nail pierced it upon a Cross
because He loves you so

You are the lamb in Jesus' arms
safe in His loving care
Because He gave His life for you
you may ever nestle there

At the Via Dolorosa

Israel Pilgrimage (2006)
John 19:16–17

Twelve feet below
the hustle and bustle and hawking
the crowds, the spices, the wares
of the present via dolorosa
lies an ancient pathway
of trodden stones
Yeshua walked upon
in sandaled feet
on His way to Calvary
2000 years ago

ancient stones
stumbling stones
stones Yeshua, weak and weary
likely fell upon as He carried
the cumbersome crossbeam
along that terrible path
to Crucifixion

I remove a shoe
to feel the coolness
of hallowed ground
against my bare sole

The Death of Messiah

We begin singing:
Were You There When They
Crucified My Lord

and *tremble*
tremble, tremble
at the reading
about the Suffering Servant
in Isaiah 53

Millenniums
seem to disappear
It almost feels
like it's happening here
now—

There's something
timeless
about it

isn't there?

THE CIRCUMCISED HEART

There was no mohel
no Brit Milah on my eighth day
no drop of blood
from my cloven heart
So, when and how it happened
cannot be pinpointed
Perhaps it occurred
when I read Moses' face shone
after he was in the presence
of the Lord, on the mountain
or that David danced
uninhibitedly before the Ark
out of impassioned love for God
or perhaps when I heard Boaz
put his covering
over the gentile Ruth
and became her kinsman redeemer
Oh, it might have been
when I made *aliyah*[16] in 1986 or 1987
or again in 2006
each time praying
at the Wall *and* the Tomb
or it may have happened

---

[16] Aliyah means ascent in Hebrew.

The Death of Messiah

upon becoming utterly awestruck
at the Little Cupula of the Tablets
or possibly the night we sang
every carol we knew
in the shepherd field of Bethlehem
It could even have been
when I drank water from
the ancient Jacob's Well
or experienced sunrise over the Dead Sea
dreaming of the Great Day
when fish will thrive
and vegetation bloom, miraculously
in its healed waters
It may well have been
the sight and smell of the land
as I walked in the footsteps
of my Jewish Savior
or when my heart
caught fire while reading
the melodious Psalms
or Solomon's *Song of Songs*
or as I poured over the account
of Peter's prison praise
Actually it probably was when
I received *blessed assurance*
that I am eternally saved
by the Blood of the Lamb...

All I know is
someway, somehow
something happened
to spiritually circumcise
this gentile heart
making it echad[17]
with the Heart of the God
of Abraham, Isaac, and Jacob
and I haven't for a single moment
been the same
since—

---

[17] Echad means one in Hebrew.

Haiku

On Ocean Grove beach
a Cross atop a sand dune
is a seagull's perch

Haiku

CHAPTER THREE

The Resurrection of Messiah

BEAUTIFUL

Matthew 27:33–66 and Matthew 28:1–6 NASB

It's not a pretty sight—
It's beautiful.
Crimson streaming
From His crown
Hands,
Side,
Feet,
Onto my head,
Flowing down my face,
Over my body,
Covering my feet,
Making me whiter than snow.

It's not a pretty sight—
It's beautiful.
It's agony.
He calls for His Father,
Writhes, gasps, thirsts.

Oh, the weighty burden
Of sin upon the Sinless One,
The world's,
Mine,
Yours.

The Resurrection of Messiah

Agony,
Ushering the covenant of salvation—
The world's,
Mine,
Yours.

It's not a pretty sight—
It's beautiful.

It is finished.

They take Him down
From the good and terrible Cross.
Hastily,
They place Him in the tomb.
Securely,
They seal the rolling stone.
They guard His grave
In awesome,
Tremulous,
Expectant
Stillness.

It's not a pretty sight—
It's beautiful.
His Body, gone.
Gone! With power
In one resplendent moment—
Seal unsealed,

Stone rolled,
Earth jolted on its axis.

Angels appear, hallowing-
Alleluia! Alleluia!
He is Risen!

We live
Because He lives.

Oh! He is beautiful.
Beautiful.

THE PLACE OF THE SKULL[18]

...O death, where is your sting?
(1 Corinthians 15:55 NASB)

Israel Pilgrimage (1987)

We gather at the base
of a mountainous rock
into which time has carved
the natural image of a human skull
... hence, its chilling name:
Place of the Skull

Above this mound lies Golgotha
where on the most significant day
in the history of the world
Jesus of Nazareth was crucified
between two thieves

I stare into the hollow eyes
of this ominous image
and am reminded of Ezekiel
and the dry bones

---

[18] There are two locations worthy of serious consideration as the place of Jesus' crucifixion and burial: the traditional site lies within the Church of the Holy Sepulcher, the other is Gordon's Calvary (Golgotha/The Place of the Skull) and the Garden Tomb (Ref. Grace Communion International).

bones that took on flesh
and blood and breath
and came to life
before his very eyes

Life.

Life is what happens at Golgotha

Life that is victorious
over the skull and bones. Victorious
over the ominous face of death

Life. Everlasting life—
for all atoned of sin

who believe

WHAT WAS GOD DOING?

*Matthew 26:36–42; Matthew 27:33–56;
and Matthew 28:1–6*

What was God doing?
What was He thinking
high up in His Heaven
when the Great Climax was unfolding
and His only begotten Son
was sweating hemorrhages of blood
in fervent prayer before Him,
that night in the garden?

What was God doing?
What was He thinking
high up in His Heaven
when His Son was pleading
for the removal of that great Grail of suffering,
yet in submission acquiesced
to His Father's higher will?

What was God doing?
What was He thinking
high up in His Heaven
during the sentencing and scourging,
spitting and mocking,

as His perfect Paschal Lamb
carried the crossbeam to Calvary,
falling and falling and falling again?
What was God doing?
What was He thinking
high up in His Heaven
when they stripped His Beloved,
held His hand to the beam and lifted the hammer
and pounded the spike through sinless flesh?
Did He hold His ears? Did He turn away?
Did His tears pour down as the blood ran down?
Did He pound His fist? Scream?

What was God doing?
What was He thinking
high up in His Heaven
when His Son cried,
Why... hast Thou... forsaken Me?
Victory was so close—
Did He almost change His mind?

What was God doing?
What was He thinking
high up in His Heaven
when it finally was finished?
Was His heavy heart throbbing
as He darkened the sky and quaked the dry earth,
opened old graves and breathed life into dead?
Was it with grief or great jubilation
that He tore asunder the curtain to the Holy of Holies?

The Resurrection of Messiah

What oh what was God thinking
at that Climax of climaxes
with Satan and sin squashed under His heel,
and after the Ascension,
at Their glorious reunion,
did Father and Son
dance the hora in Highest Heaven?

It's No Wonder

Luke 8:1–2; Matthew 27:55–56; and John 20:1–18

It's no wonder
Mary of Magdala
traveled with Rabboni
and the twelve
and helped
support His mission
She was a woman on fire
with love and gratitude
a woman freed
of seven snarling demons

It's no wonder
despite trepidation
she watched at a distance
as they nailed her Great One
to a wretched cross
cupping her ears, wailing
at each resonating hammer fall
No wonder
she drew near
as He hung
in the agony of dying
for being there

The Resurrection of Messiah

was better
than not being there

Mary, bereft
looked upon her Rabboni
as they took Him
from the beams
laid His powerless Body
in the tomb
and rolled a great round stone
across the entrance
separating Him from her
before the sun went down
that Good and terrible Friday

and it's no wonder
she was back at dawn
the morning after Sabbath
with other ministering women
carrying spices
heedless of who
would roll the stone away

But the tomb was open
and the women trembled
as an angel astounded them
with talk of rising

Behold the Lamb...Poetically!

Bewildered
Mary ran to the apostles
but it's no wonder
she returned
to grieve near the tomb,
wanting to be
where last He was

A stranger, *the gardener?*
inquired of her weeping
Sir, she implored
*if you have carried Him away
tell me where you have put Him
and I will get Him*

Mary...

Rabboni!

Astonished, she reflexively
reached for Him...

Do not cling to Me
He told her

*for I have not yet ascended
to My Father*

The Resurrection of Messiah

Oh, it's no wonder
it was she He entrusted
to bring the news
to the brethren
No wonder
she ran, stumbling over rocks
and potsherd
dashing through brush
and brambles
raising tufts of dust
eager to exclaim
breathless with jubilation

I have seen the Lord!

MARY OF MAGDALA

Luke 8:1–2; Matthew 27:55–56; and John 20:1–18

Mary of Magdala was privileged—

Like the disciples, she was among the few
who spent time with Jesus, followed Him
considered Him Teacher and Friend
She called Him, Rabboni

Mary had lived in darkness with demons
Jesus rid her of their terror
drew her into the Light
and she was grateful
She and the brethren experienced
the wonder of unconditional love
from He, Who personified it, perfectly

No doubt Mary was there
when Jesus spoke of things
the multitudes yearned to know
like living the beatitudes
like eternity, death, and resurrection
like the prophetic sign of Jonah

The Resurrection of Messiah

Still, neither she nor the disciples
had a clear understanding
of cosmic events that were about to unfold

Then suddenly everything whirled
out of their control
Palm branch homage
hosannas and hallelujahs
quickly turned to betrayal
abduction and a mockery of a trial

There were thunderous shouts of

Crucify Him! Crucify Him!

It was no longer safe
on the streets of Jerusalem
for His followers. They became fearful
Some went into hiding

Then, Jesus was Crucified—
The earth quaked
and the sky went dark

Mary rent her garments and wailed
Full of sorrow, what could she do
except go early the day after the Sabbath
to anoint His dead body

But when she arrived at the tomb
it was empty and His body was gone
Angels were there—
resplendent angels, who spoke of resurrection

Mary was weeping, utterly bewildered
She couldn't grasp resurrection—
All she could wonder was
Where was her Teacher's body?
Who took His body away?

Suddenly, Rabboni appeared to her
He called her, tenderly by name, but
she couldn't comprehend
that Him standing there, speaking to her
could possibly be true—
He was dead. Wasn't He?

Mary was struggling to fathom
that the greatest knowledge
ever to befall anyone, anytime, anywhere
befell upon her at that amazing moment

This wasn't a time for weeping—
This was time for rejoicing!

She extended her hand to touch Him—

The Resurrection of Messiah

He was Alive! Breathing!
Warm! With flesh and bones—
Indeed, *He had risen from the grave!*

Jesus told her to tell His disciples
so Mary quickly hurried off, proclaiming

I have seen the Lord!

Oh! It was starting to sink in—
The sin of the world was atoned for
by Jesus' death on the Cross
and by His glorious Resurrection
He became the Firstfruits
of Life Forevermore!

Alleluia! Alleluia! Alleluia!

I'VE READ THE END OF THE BOOK

Twice I heard Tony Campolo[19] deliver
his famous and rousing sermon
"It's Friday, but Sunday's Comin'!"
at The Great Auditorium in Ocean Grove
Tony drummed home the point
that everything may look bleak on Friday, but…
come Sunday… Sunday changes everything!

Now, I'm not thinking of just any dark and bleak
    Friday
I'm thinking about the original *Good* Friday—
thinking the only reason I can bear
to contemplate that good and terrible day
is because I know
a few days later there was
a mind-blowing, miraculous Sunday—
… Resurrection Sunday!

The disciples didn't have
the advantage I have—
They didn't understand
life after death

---

[19] Anthony "Tony" Campolo is an American sociologist, pastor, author, public speaker, and former spiritual advisor to US President Bill Clinton (Wikipedia).

The Resurrection of Messiah

couldn't comprehend
atonement for sin
just didn't get it
that their teacher and friend, Jesus,
could die upon a cross
to atone for the sins of the world
They didn't realize
they were in the middle of miracles
Didn't know the future—
Sure, they may have read portions of the Scrolls
but they didn't have the whole wonderful Book

I do have the whole Book
I've read ahead
and studied the pages
I know that what follows
the sorrowful, tear-generating
Good Friday story
is the victorious hope-giving
hallelujah happy ending

I know my sins are forgiven
know I'm going to live forever
Yes, I know what happened next
and that makes all the difference

A VERY PERSONAL BLESSING
Israel Pilgrimage (2006)

Bob and I sit meditatively
on a bench in the pastoral garden
in view of the Garden Tomb—
Our pilgrimage is almost over
In a few hours we'll prepare
for the long flight home

I catch a glimpse of a bookstore
and am jolted into remembering
that one of my poems
"Extraordinary Matzoh"
published in William Francis' book
Celebrate the Feasts of the Lord[20]
may actually be for sale, here
at the Garden Tomb

so we go inside—
and sure enough, see it
beckoning to me from the shelf
among so many other
interesting and inviting holy books

---

[20] *Celebrate the Feasts of the Lord* by William W. Francis. Crest Books, Salvation Army National Publications, 1997.

The Resurrection of Messiah

I reach for a copy
even though I have one at home
(except this one
has a label printed in Hebrew
and a price tag in shekels)
So, whether it is silly or frivolous
I approach the cashier to pay

and swipe my hand across
the smooth russet cover that depicts
a glowing hanukiah and a scroll
then flip through pages
to find what I know
is on page 31... *my poem*
introducing the chapter
about the Feast of Unleavened Bread

Oh! It blesses my soul
to discover my own simple words
here at this sacred spot
Truly, it blesses my soul to know
even when I return home today
books that contain this earnest poem of praise
will remain as my gift of blessing to the Land

Extraordinary Matzoh[21]

It's only ordinary unleavened bread
Ordinary matzoh
On an earthen plate
It probably came
From a supermarket shelf
A Manischewitz box
Ordinary matzoh
Blessed for Passover
Oh, but when I take it
And cradle it lovingly
In my hands
Break it and bless it
It is for me
Most Holy Bread
Good Friday Bread
Body of the Lamb that was slain
With my cup of Redemption
Communion Bread
Lechem[22] without hametz[23]
Without yeast of sin
Pierced

---

[21] Matzoh is the Hebrew word for unleavened bread.

[22] Lechem is the Hebrew word for bread.

[23] Hametz is the Hebrew word for leaven.

The Resurrection of Messiah

Striped
Bruised
Shrouded afikomen[24]
Hidden
Then resurrected
With glory
I partake
Alleluia, alleluia
Alleluia, alleluia, alleluia!

---

[24] Afikomen is the Hebrew word for the hidden matzoh.

A Better Idea

It's a better idea than spring baskets,
with jelly beans, mallows, and bows;
it's far better than flowery straw bonnets,
Mary Janes and brand new clothes.

A much better idea than bunnies and chicks,
eggs painted pink, purple, blue...
This time let us give our sweet children
an Easter gift that will ring true.

Let's give a plush lamb, all spotless and pure
and tell them Jesus is its name...
Tell them Jesus is the Hope of the World
and Easter's the reason He came.

Tell them God's Son is sinless and meek
He's the unblemished Passover Lamb;
tell them He died on Calvary's Cross
to save sinners. He's the great I Am.

Tell them that on the first Easter morning
Lamb Jesus arose from the grave—
and that is why in their tiny hands
is the soft little lamb that you gave.

The Resurrection of Messiah

Tell them Lord Jesus loves them so much
that He wants to be their Best Friend.
Their little lamb will remind them of Him
after Resurrection Day ends.

Tell them chocolate bunnies, bonnets, and beans
are okay, but not the best part—
the best part of Easter is Jesus, the Lamb,
Who came to live in their hearts!

HE IS NOT HERE
Israel Pilgrimage (2006)

Some believe
the Body of Messiah was placed
in the highly venerated
tomb located in the Church
of the Holy Sepulcher

Some believe
He was buried
in a pastoral place
known as the Garden Tomb

The important thing is—
He died. He rose.
He'll come again.

The important thing is
as a placard proclaims
at the entrance
to the Garden Tomb:

He is not here—
He is risen from the dead

The Resurrection of Messiah

and the important thing is
our sins are atoned—

We live because He lives

so there's nothing
left to say, except

Hallelujah!

Praise be to Jesus, Our Risen Savior!

BEHOLD THE MAN

There's an archway in Jerusalem, engraved with the words, "Ecce Homo," which represents the place where Pontius Pilate paraded Jesus, bloody and bedraggled, before the hostile crowd, and exclaimed, "Behold the Man!"

JOHN 19:5

I. Behold Him

The King of all kings, downcast
among those He came to save
wearing a robe, stained red
crowned with a branch
of twisted thorns
clenching a brittle reed—
His royal scepter
in His royal right hand

as Blood trickles
down His brow
spittle drips
down His chin
His eyes
are puffed and dazed
His strength, gone

THE RESURRECTION OF MESSIAH

He stands
amid those He loves
those He came to save—
mocked, scourged, silent
silent as a docile lamb
He is the Docile Lamb

A multitude—
the very people He loves
cry out in unison

Crucify Him!

Soldiers lead Him
stumbling and falling
to the crucifixion site
the ominous Place of the Skull—

They pound nails
through cringing flesh
and post the charge
above His thorn-crowned head
further mocking Him
with *Truth*—

*This is Jesus
the King of the Jews*

II. Behold Him

In the fullness of time
This Once-Mocked King will return
crowned with beauty and majesty
to reign—

hallowed with Hallelujahs
and Hosannas

Multitudes will gaze
with wondrous awe
upon the Risen One
the One they pierced, returned

A multitude of knees
will fall to the dirt, and kneel
as countless tongues proclaim
with resounding adoration:

Jesus is Lord!

and this once ridiculed, bedraggled
crucified Savior King
will be hailed in Heaven and on Earth
by men and by angels
as Our King of all kings forever—
and ever and ever

with Alleluias earnest

… at last!

HOLY FACE
Luke 24:12

When I look upon Your Visage
and pierced, bruised Body
imprinted upon the winding sheet,
and contemplate
wounds You bore for me,
it causes me to quiver
with reverence and awe.
After two millennia
I witness Your Passion
mapped out
on a white linen proof sheet.

Controversy has abounded
about the authenticity
of this ancient Shroud of Turin;
I leave it to greater minds
than mine to ponder.
As for me,
in my spirit I know,
it is You, my Lord.
Amazing. I can look
upon the negative
that's positive
and actually see Your Face,

Behold the Lamb...Poetically!

Your beautiful Holy Face,
suspended from Its Divine Agony
and interlude with death
when Your Majestic Imprint
burst upon the burial cloth.
Death sprang to Life
in that timeless flash-moment
of Resurrection. *Glorious!*

Lord, I see Strength,
unimaginable Endurance,
but even more, Peace
and the Countenance
of Unsurpassed Love.

Others may debate carbon dating.
Let them scrutinize and snip,
analyze in test tubes,
on smeared slides under microscopes,
and beneath glaring, blaring lights
until Your Second Coming!

As for me,
when I gaze into the negative
that's positive
burnished miraculously
into that Holy Shroud
at the *Climax* of all time,
I accept with simple faith,
it is You, my Lord.

INVISIBLE DESECRATIONS
JERUSALEM HOLY PLACES

Israel Pilgrimage (1986)

I.

After waiting patiently
in a solemn line
amid gold and glow
jeweled icons
and pungent incense
she prayerfully descends
with prepared heart
into the Empty Tomb
beneath the Church
of the Holy Sepulcher
for one mind-blowingly
sacred moment
of her lifetime

A black-garbed priest
thrusts a candle at her—

One dollar!

Appalled at intrusion
even sacrilege

she reflexively
rummages for a bill
ignites the wick
salvages a split second
of holy observance
of the rough-hewn slab
where the body
of her Savior lay
until that awesome
Resurrection Morning

Turning to leave
she catches sight
of the priest
extinguishing her taper
preparing to sell it again
to the unsuspecting pilgrim
next in line

II.

At the women's side
of the Western Wall
she tightly folds
her fervent plea
written to God
on a bit of paper
and tucks it
as mortar
well into a crevice
She stands

The Resurrection of Messiah

shoulder to shoulder
with devout sisters
native and foreign
touches the cool
ancient stones
smoothed
by multitudinous hands
and beseeches, softly
earnestly
in the Spirit
her Abba Father
prayer language
blending Pentecostally
with holy Hebrew
and tongues
of distant lands

Suddenly
a pointed finger
jabs her shoulder:

*A donation, please,
for the Yeshiva*

She reflexively
rummages for a bill
then reaches
for the wall
trying to remember
where she left off

Yeshua[25]

Yeshua
Yes You are
The Miraculous Offspring
Of I AM

Yeshua
Yes You are
The Paschal
Lamb

Yeshua
Our Atonement
Flowed down
Crossed
Wooden beams

Surrendered Life
Became
Our Great Salvation

Yes it did
Suffering Servant

---

[25] Yeshua in Hebrew is a verbal derivative from "to rescue," "to deliver". It is the name of Jesus.

THE RESURRECTION OF MESSIAH

Lion of Judah
Sar ha Shalom[26]

Yeshua
Yes You are
HaMashiach[27]

Yes!

You Are.

---

[26] Sar ha Shalom is Hebrew for Prince of Peace.

[27] HaMashiach in Hebrew means "The Anointed One." Yeshua HaMashiach means Jesus, the Messiah.

Risen

It's Holy Saturday

Dough is rising
on the kitchen counter

filling me with thoughts
of rising

helium balloons
set free

sunrise
over the Sea of Galilee

waking up

rising

soap bubbles
floating skyward

seagulls soaring

fireworks
booming and bursting

The Resurrection of Messiah

jet planes at takeoff

rocket ships
with long trails of fire
zooming to the moon

O, but nothing

nowhere

and no one

has ever done it

or will

... like Jesus

THE EMMAUS TRIPTYCH
Luke 24:13–35

I. The Unnamed Friend

Cleopas and friend walked and talked
with lumbering gaits and downcast faces
shining hopes of sweet redemption
dashed and obliterated

They asked of each other the why question
for if *anyone* had come to fill those old prophecies
surely it had seemed to be Him
that Jesus they'd come to know
through signs and wonders
that *appeared* to be miraculous

Their so-called Messiah had been crucified,
was dead and gone. Yes, gone, gone, gone!
Even His cold dead body was missing
from the tomb that had been sealed—

He approached them
in the midst of their perplexity
on the road to Emmaus
He walked with them, talked with them

The Resurrection of Messiah

they even felt His fire
but didn't know who He was

and strange as that may seem
how often have I been
the unnamed friend of Cleopas?
I, too, profess to know Him, know Him well
yet fail to recognize Him along the road

II. The Stranger

Taking the barley loaf in his hands
the stranger lifted it

Baruch ata Adonai
Eloheynu Melech ha Olam
ha motzie lechem
min ha'aretz[28]

He tore it, offered it, and just as it fell
into reaching grasps
their astonished eyes recognized Him
and in that instant
He utterly vanished from their sight!

Leaping from the table, Cleopas and his friend
stumbled over each other
looking under, over, around and around

---

[28] The Blessing Over the Bread: We praise You, Eternal God, Sovereign of the universe, Who brings forth bread from the earth.

knowing even as they did
it was True after all

As they looked at each other
their disbelief became relief
the sweet awakening of a deep Belief

for Truth visited *them* along the way
joined them at their table, broke their humble bread
They asked each other:

*Were not our hearts burning
as He talked with us on the road
and opened the Scriptures to us?*
Now, blazing temples of Holy Fire
they suddenly knew their once-shattered hearts
would never cool again

III. My Emmaus

When I first found You, or You found me
I thought I'd go from strength to strength
pinnacle to pinnacle, joy to joy
and so it was for a season
when love was new

Then the whirlwind came
thrashing through my world
upending all my securities
leaving me stunned, broken, alone
certain I would die

THE RESURRECTION OF MESSIAH

So I waited for You to save me
waited for prayers pleaded at Your scarred feet
to avail their just reward
for I believed in You, trusted, hoped
Eyes veiled, I couldn't find You
failed to recognize You along the road

Had I believed in vain?

Then You began to speak
not audibly, but whenever I opened Your Word
Radiance, Glory, Unfailing Love
sprang from the page and became manifest
My heart blazed! I began to shine!

Now, on the other side of sorrow
I dare not forget my burning heart,
Your Glorious Presence
so I abide, remembering
it is You, my Jesus
Who walks with me along the road

ALONG EMMAUS ROAD
Luke 24 and Isaiah 53 NASB

I'm sitting in the kitchen
with my Bible open
reading about the men
who were walking to Emmaus
the Sunday following the Crucifixion

thinking how bewildered they were
and dismayed that the One
they supposed was their Savior was gone—
He died upon that Cross on Friday
leaving their hopes completely dashed

and I'm thinking about Jesus
joining them on their journey
as a complete stranger
bringing the hope of the Gospel
as He explained about Himself in the Tanakh[29]
without revealing that they were actually walking
the seven miles to Emmaus
with their newly Resurrected Lord
I flip through the pages
and see *Jesus* handwritten in the margins

---

[29] Tanakh is the Hebrew Bible.

The Resurrection of Messiah

of the Old Testament, over and over
wherever I've discovered Him anew
and recall each exciting revelation

and imagine their amazement
as they listened to Jesus
revealing Himself as He spoke
about Moses and the Prophets
particularly when He came to the part
about the Suffering Servant in Isaiah 53
How exciting it had to have been to hear it
from the lips of the Suffering Servant, Himself—

Despised and forsaken
a man of sorrows, acquainted with grief
smitten of God and afflicted
pierced for our transgressions
crushed for our iniquities
by whose scourging we were healed

Who like a lamb was led to the slaughter
Who like a sheep, was silent before its shearers

assigned a grave with wicked men
but was with a rich man in death

He rendered Himself as a guilt offering
and God would prolong His days

Behold the Lamb...Poetically!

Jesus... Jesus... Jesus

I visualize the men
clutching their burning hearts

When they reached their destination
they invited the stranger to stay with them
because the hour was late

and as they gathered around a table
to partake of an evening meal
Jesus lifted a loaf to bless—

Suddenly their eyes beheld
His nail-pierced hands!
and as He broke their humble bread
they recognized Him

In that instant *Jesus vanished!*

but the words He spoke
along the road that day
were permanently seared
upon their burning hearts

so they rose from the table
and hurried off that very hour
all the way back to Jerusalem, *in the dark*
to tell the disciples of all the wonders
that happened that remarkable day

SUNFLOWERS ALONG EMMAUS ROAD
Israel Pilgrimage (1986)
Luke 24:13–35 NASB

A field of big, bodacious sunflowers
remind me of a great cathedral choir
singing the *Hallelujah Chorus*
with exultation
while sun-shining millions
of dazzling petal spires upon us
along Emmaus Road

It is fitting
because I am ablaze
with Jesus-joy
to be here

as I think about my newly
Resurrected Lord, *vanishing*
at the very breaking
of the bread

astonishing the disciples
who sat with Him
at the table

Behold the Lamb...Poetically!

Those utterly bewildered disciples
whose hearts thumped
and blazed
with glory fire
as He walked with them
as He explained to them
the Holy Scriptures

2000 years ago
somewhere
along this very road

WHAT IS TRUTH?
John 18:38 NASB

I first learned
the importance of truth
at my mother's knee
My children
learned it at mine

Life has taught me
truth is truth, even
if no one believes it
if no one wants to believe it
if every man is a liar

What's true is true, even
if millions are spent
to disprove it
if it's argued against
lobbied against
debated against
railed against
voted against
legislated against

Truth Is

absolute—

even if it's watered down
to make it acceptable
skirted around
to soften its appeal
lubed with oil
so it goes down
nice and easy
sugarcoated
to make it palatable

even if it looks
soooo, soooo good

Truth is Truth
whether it's popular
or unpopular

... even
in the face
of persecution

Pilate asked,
What is truth?

The Resurrection of Messiah

The Psalmist wrote,
The sum of God's word
is truth

Jesus said,
I Am the Truth

He also said,
Everyone on the side
of truth
listens to Me

I believe the supreme
Truth is a Man
and His unchanging Word

... even though
He be crucified

Jesus—
Salvation Truth
Resurrection Truth
Living Truth

Truth—
I can stand up for

God's Unfathomable Love

*For God so loved the world, that He gave His
only begotten Son, that whoever believes in Him
shall not perish, but have eternal life.*
(John 3:16 NASB)

For God—
The Majestic Almighty, Omnipotent, King of Kings
Ancient of Days, Elohim, Adonai
my beloved Abba Father

so loved—
with the bigness of His gracious agape heart
a love unfathomable, unconditional
and abounding in mercy

the world—
the whole wide world and everyone in it
in Israel, Jordan, Iran, Russia, Nigeria, China
in Ireland and Italy, where my ancestors came from
in Hochhausen, Germany, where loved ones reside
where we've been on vacation, Aruba and Bermuda
and all of us right here, in Wayne, New Jersey

The Resurrection of Messiah

that He gave His only begotten Son—
given to us, freely, our Father's extraordinary gift
of Yeshua/Jesus, His sinless Son,
to save us from punishment we deserve
for sins we have committed

that whoever believes in Him—
so all we need do to receive this wondrous gift
is believe God's trustworthy Word
believe that Jesus was born into the world
and that He is our promised Savior

shall not perish—
because of Jesus' sacrifice upon Calvary's Tree
and because His Most Precious Blood
atoned for all our sins
death has been swallowed up in victory!

but have eternal life—
because of Jesus' miraculous
resurrection from death
we live because He lives
and will dwell with Him
in the Kingdom of Heaven
to enjoy unimaginable splendors
forever... forevermore
Praise the Lord!

Acts, Chapter 2

Sometimes—
when I read my Bible
I imagine myself
there, in the rumpled, dog-eared pages
where and when remarkable things
were happening

For instance—
Oh, I wish I could've been
in the room that morning in Jerusalem
on the Day of Pentecost
when an astonishing sound
of rushing wind came from Heaven
and filled the place with the Holy Spirit

wish I could've been among
the crowd of bewildered people
clutching garments and belongings
securing food baskets and money bags
amid the sound of whirring wind
wondering what was going on
I would've seen with startled eyes
blazing tongues of fire appear
then split and rest above us all
would've heard the Galileans

The Resurrection of Messiah

miraculously uttering languages
they did not know
proclaiming good news
to people of every nation

Oh, joy! Euphoria!

I would've heard
preposterous ridicule and accusations
that we were drunk with wine
Drunk with wine so early in the morning!

Had I been there, I would've seen
Peter stand with his brethren
and quote the prophet Joel
and speak of Jesus
Crucifixion, Resurrection
and call us to repent

and finally, would've witnessed
three thousand souls receive salvation
and I would've been in that number

Oh! How great that would've been
How exciting to imagine

but, I didn't need to be there
God had other plans—

Behold the Lamb...poetically!

On another Holy Pentecost
His Spirit came to rest on me
just as surely as it did
on the early believers
in Jerusalem, that day

and just the same as they
I have been changed

forever

Hallelujah Hands

I want men everywhere to lift up holy hands in prayer, without anger or disputing.

(1 Timothy 2:8 NIV)

Some lift one
others both
chest high, chin high
Some reach upward
ceilingward, skyward
stretching Heavenward
reaching for
His hem

Soft, young graceful hands
with squared airbrushed fingertips
Pudgy, fidgety, child hands
copying his daddy hands
Brown hands, pale hands
old bulging vein hands
Just plain hands
hands with bands
hands flashing rings
stones sparkling
Calloused hands, splintered hands
rough, red dishpan hands

Cold hands, warm hands
peanut butter and jelly hands
Salon hands
nails lacquered red
rose pink or pearly

Tambourine shaking
banner waving
clap clapping
Bible clutching
baby holding
tear wiping
clenching, wrenching
God beseeching hands

Hands clasping the hand
of another
hands signing praise
for ears that cannot hear
hands folded
serenely in a lap
All beautiful
all holy
all His children's
hallelujah hands

Mount Scopus
Israel Pilgrimage (2006)

It's nighttime—
We arrive at Mount Scopus
overlooking Yerushalayim[30]
The stars glimmer
in the heavens
and The City is lit up
like the jewel of all the earth

Wishful, I want
there to be fireworks
want the surroundings
to express the excitement
stirring inside of me—
Suddenly, I hear
the unmistakable sound of fireworks
boom, boom, booming
somewhere
although I cannot see
the luminous splendors
bursting in the sky
We partake of the fruit of the vine—
our cup of blessing
as we prepare to enter in

---

[30] Yerushalayim is the Hebrew word for Jerusalem

Behold the Lamb...poetically!

Our rabbi prays
for the peace of Jerusalem
prays the Shema[31]
prays the Shehekianu[32]
covers his head
with a magnificent tallit[33]
embellished with
the Star of David and the Lamb
then he lifts his hands and prays
the Aaronic Benediction

Our joy cannot be contained—
This is the City of Our Great King

I watch a tear
trickle down
my rabbi's face

---

[31] The Shema is the central prayer in the Jewish prayer book (siddur).

[32] The Shehekianu is a common Jewish prayer to celebrate special occasions.

[33] Prayer shawl

Marco Sounds the Shofar
Israel Pilgrimage (2006)

Marco bought a shofar in Galilee—
a long and spiraled Yemenite shofar
made from the horn
of a kudu antelope

With a deep and steady breath
Marco blows its harrowing thunder
over the Mount of Olives
the Western Wall
the Jordan River
and just about every site
we visit in holy Zion

trumpeting its long distinctive wail
to jolt us from our complacency—

Wake up!

Warning all hearers:

Prepare! Repent!

Behold the Lamb...Poetically!

Wake up! Oh Sleepers—
Wake up! and follow the Lord, Our God!

Anne brought her tambourine
from New Jersey—
It's shaped like a Star of David
Colorful ribbons stream
from its six points

Like Miriam, Anne lifts it high
and dances with delight
praising Adonai with worshipful women
from all over the world
as their swirling skirts sweep the ground
It's Shabbat, in Jerusalem
at the Western Wall

and I bought a tallit in Tiberius—
blue and white like the Israeli flag
with knotted fringes in the corners
to remind me God's promises are true
a traditional prayer shawl
to wrap snuggly around my shoulders
like God's loving arms
enfolding me
as I pray

THE LITTLE CUPOLA OF THE TABLETS
Israel Pilgrimage (2006)

If it is true
as I've heard said
that this little spot
on the Temple Mount
is the actual place
where Abraham
bound his son,
the location
of the Most Holy Place
in the Holy of Holies
and the very same spot
where Jesus
will return

If this is amazingly so...
this would be
the most hallowed ground
on earth

... so I remove my sandals
and feel the sublime coolness
on my humble soles

BEHOLD THE LAMB...POETICALLY!

Maria picks up
a tiny chip of ancient stone
tinier than a pea—

She gives it to me
to keep

THERE ARE NO WORDS
My Love Poem to Jesus

Sometimes, there are no words—

I come before You, Lord, with adoration
filled with a strong desire to express my love
but all the words that come to mind
seem overused and feeble
and cannot convey what I long to say

I'm a poet, a wordsmith
with adjectives aplenty, and
dictionaries, thesauruses, lexicons
close at hand, but
today I yearn to bless You afresh
with eloquence, depth, and originality
I want it to be profound
something You've never heard before
however, I find there are no words
none to express the inexpressible

So I empty myself of words
and call upon Your Spirit
Sounds begin to tumble off my tongue
and through my lips

Behold the Lamb...Poetically!

I trust a perfect utterance
rises like incense to Your throne
that is pleasing to Your ears

Then I simply sit awhile
awestruck in silence
arms lifted heavenward
and let my beating heart speak
the unspeakable

content that You know
how much I love You, Lord

I Can't Make You Love Him

I can't make you love Him if you don't
Can't strike a match
to cause your heart to blaze
at the mention of His Name
can't cause you to tremble
as I tremble
before His holiness
can't jump-start love
from the outside in
It only happens from the inside out

No matter how much I love you

loving Him
is not something you can get from me
like a cup of mulled cider or a hug
not something you can inherit
like good genes, strong teeth, or curly hair
not something I can demonstrate
like how to knead dough or rhyme couplets
nor is it something I can gift wrap
tie with a crimson ribbon
and give you to make you happy

Behold the Lamb...Poetically!

No, all I can do is tell the old, old story
about His beauty, as I perceive it
His mercy, as I've experienced it
His wonders and His love
All I can do is hope, pray,
and wait

Truth will not impose
Truth waits to be sought
Answers wait for age-old questions
The Door waits for your knock

When He opens
You'll find He's been expecting you
already loving you

No, I can't make it easy, although it can be
I embarked on my quest; you'll embark on yours
No, I can't make you love Him if you don't
but should your quest lead you to His heart
I'll be waiting, like the One inside the door
to dance in the glow of His grandeur with you

MESSIANIC BELIEVERS AND ORTHODOX JEWS AT THE WESTERN WALL

Israel Pilgrimage (2006)

We sing like David sang
dance like David danced—
Tambourines, timbrels, and delight—
It's Erev Shabbat at the Western Wall

Lifting our hands in heartfelt praise
to Yeshua, Messiah
we stand on holy ground
upon the very stones
He may once have walked upon

as the Orthodox women dance
their circle dance of joy
worshipping Adonai
their long skirts sweeping
the smooth ancient stones
their countenances shining with smiles
in Sabbath celebration

as the Orthodox men
garbed head to toe in black
read holy words in holy books

while others sway rhythmically in prayer
or reach to touch the towering wall

as enthusiastic young men
run forward, shouting
for the coming of

Mashiach! Mashiach! Mashiach![34]

O Lord have mercy upon us—
We suppress the burning yearning
to grab a bullhorn and a soapbox
to proclaim what we know is true:

*Mashiach has come
and His Name is Yeshua!*

We may not know ourselves
if it is out of respect
so as not to antagonize
or our own personal cowardice—
that we speak not a word

---

[34] Mashiach is the Hebrew word for Messiah.

The Watchman

Perhaps the Mashiach
is on His way,
ready
to lead us
to the Promised Land.
There have been signs
of His coming
that haven't been reported
in the papers
or radio or TV newscasts.

I'm a watchman.
I wait.
I prepare,
knowing not
the Day or the Hour.
I plant my rose bush
at the gate,
sup,
rinse my bowl,
retire—
trying to live
His Great Command
as best I can.

Perhaps He'll come
tomorrow.
It's possible.

Wonderful News

I have to share the most wonderful news with those I love most in this world.

The news I have is more precious, by far, than diamonds or rubies or gold.

There was an enormous void in my life. "Is this all there is?" I would ask.

I searched far to find some meaning in life. It seemed an unknowable task.

One day someone shared the Gospel with me, and I learned that Jesus is real.

I prayed to invite Him into my heart and was filled with astonishing zeal!

The day that He gave His life on the Cross, to save all mankind from our sin,

He opened to us salvation by grace; life eternal, the prize that we win.

The Resurrection of Messiah

You know that I share the best that I have with my cherished family and friends,

so listen, dear one, to this wonderful news upon which ever after depends.

Just open your Bible to the Gospel of John, third chapter, verse number three,

then read of God's love in the sixteenth verse to learn what has happened to me.

Some people grow up with Bible in hand, without Jesus burning in heart,

some haven't explored the true meaning of life; some wouldn't know where to start.

Whether you're Protestant, Jewish, my friend, Catholic, Muslim, atheist,

my news is for you and all who will hear, who long to receive of God's best.

You needn't become a fanatic or prude, I've no list of do nots and dos.

God's Spirit will teach you all you need know. The offer's too good to refuse.

Although tribulation may take you by storm and trials may bring a hard test,

God's greater, He's faithful, He'll bring you through to victory. You'll shine in His rest.

This can be the greatest day of your life, the day you receive the New Birth.

This can be the day you begin to know why we're the happiest people on earth.

Like me, you will yearn to share the Good News with all of the people you love.

Like me, you will want all those you meet to be touched by our Great God above.

BIOGRAPHY

Maude Carolan Pych is a former newspaper reporter who now writes Christian inspirational poetry and poems to record family history. She raised her family amid the picturesque mountains, lakes, and reservoirs of Ringwood, NJ, in the 1970s.

Her love for poetry began when as a teenager she was introduced to the poetry of Edgar Allen Poe, John Masefield, Edna St. Vincent Millay, and Gerard Manley Hopkins. She was enthralled by sounds of clanging bells in Poe's "The Bells" and of the sea in Masefield's "Sea Fever." She studied music, taking lessons to play marimba, piano, clarinet, and drums, and as an adult, gradually developed an interest in the wonderful music of words.

One of the first poems Maude wrote as an adult was a rhyme entitled "The Narrowest." It was about walking the narrow path as a follower of Jesus. While sitting on the edge of her bed with a legal pad in hand, the words came almost faster than she could write. When she came to the end, she read it aloud and wept. She'd been praying for a way to minister God's love, and suddenly the path before her became clear.

During her third pilgrimage to Israel in 2006, she and her

husband were sitting on a bench by the Garden Tomb, which many believe to be the burial place of Jesus. Suddenly she remembered that a book in which one of her poems "Extraordinary Matzoh" was published was for sale in the bookstore there. The book, *Celebrate the Feasts of the Lord* is by William W. Francis. They hurried in, saw it and its price tag in shekels, and purchased it, and she was delighted that one of her simple poems of praise was available at one of the holiest places on earth.

Maude has taken part in several retreats and workshops conducted by poets Maria Mazziotti Gillan and Laura Boss. She's a four-time finalist and recipient of Editor's Choice Awards in the Allen Ginsberg Poetry Contest. Maude has also won awards at the St. Catherine of Bologna Festival of the Arts in Ringwood, NJ. Her work has appeared in publications including *The Paterson Literary Review*, *Sensations Magazine*, *Lips*, *The Pillar Monthly*, and William W. Francis' book and has also been included in anthologies about the city of Paterson (NJ) and the *Jersey Shore*. A member of the North Jersey Christian Writers Group and Ringwood Manor Association of the Arts, the poet regularly posts to her blog, *Maude's Poems* at: http://maudespoems.com.

Maude has published *Wonderhoods*, a 411-page memoir in poetry, available on her website, and created six chapbooks: *The Circumcised Heart*, *Bliss*, *From My Heart to Yours at Christmas—Cookies & Poems*, *The Widow's Song*, *A Pilgrim's Quest—A Poet Visits the Holy Land*, and *God's Square Mile—Poems about Ocean Grove*.

A mother and grandmother, the poet resides in northern New Jersey with her husband and most ardent encourager, Robert F. Pych. They attend Beth Israel Worship Center/The Jerusalem Center in Wayne, NJ, where Maude serves as a deaconess.

www.ingramcontent.com/pod-product-compliance
Lightning Source LLC
Jackson TN
JSHW030406151025
92573JS00014B/540